Carmela C. Maresca is president of The Maresca/Wolff Organization, Inc., a New York-based "think tank" specializing in the development and implementation of marketing, sales, and promotion strategies. The author of numerous magazine articles, including a monthly column in *Ad Age* titled "Outthinking the Competition," Ms. Maresca is a former member of President Carter's Taskforce on Women in Business and the coordinator of the nation's first "Women in Business" week.

CAREERS IN MARKETING
A Woman's Guide

Carmela C. Maresca

A SPECTRUM BOOK

PRENTICE-HALL, INC., Englewood Cliffs, New Jersey 07632

Library of Congress Cataloging in Publication Data

Maresca, Carmela.
    Careers in marketing; a woman's guide.

    "A Spectrum Book."
    Includes index.
    1. Women in marketing.   2. Marketing—Vocational
guidance.   I. Title.
HF5415.122.M37   1983   658.8'0023'73   82-21482
ISBN 0-13-115139-8
ISBN 0-13-115121-5 (pbk.)

This book is available at a special discount when ordered
in bulk quantities. Contact Prentice-Hall, Inc., General
Publishing Division, Special Sales, Englewood Cliffs, N.J. 07632.

ISBN 0-13-115139-8

ISBN 0-13-115121-5 {PBK.}

A SPECTRUM BOOK

10   9   8   7   6   5   4   3   2   1

Printed in the United States of America

Manufacturing buyer Christine Johnston
Cover design © 1983 by Jeannette Jacobs

Prentice-Hall International, Inc., *London*
Prentice-Hall of Australia Pty. Limited, *Sydney*
Prentice-Hall of Canada Inc., *Toronto*
Prentice-Hall of India Private Limited, *New Delhi*
Prentice-Hall of Japan, Inc., *Tokyo*
Prentice-Hall of Southeast Asia Pte. Ltd., *Singapore*
Whitehall Books Limited, *Wellington, New Zealand*
Editora Prentice-Hall do Brasil Ltda., *Rio de Janeiro*

Contents

II

NEW DIRECTIONS IN MARKETING

6

Marketing for the Nonprofit Organization, 57

7

Marketing for the Professional Service Organization, 64

III

EMBARKING ON A MARKETING CAREER

8

Strategy for Embarking on a Career in Marketing, 77

Preface

Approximately 44 million American women are in the work force today. This single statistic, more than any other, indicates what the future holds. It is a reshaped, redirected society we live in. For better or worse, it will never again be the same. Although inequities in pay for like-occupations continue to exist for women, sexism continues to show its immature face, and sexual pressures and sexual politics will most probably always be with us. The clear direction of women's role in the business and marketing functions of the 1980s and beyond is unmistakably set.

This book is the result of over twenty years of experience in the marketing world. By necessity, this book broadly reviews various elements of marketing, and it is written not as a text for learning the academic equations of marketing but as a guide to handling the very real and sometimes unusual situations confronting women in the world of marketing and business in general. There are many benefits to women in the world of marketing. I sincerely hope that the student of marketing, whatever her age or station in life, will use this book to provide personal insight into problem solving with a woman's touch and will use it as a pleasant addition to supplement more formal reading. It is also hoped that reader enlightenment will result in a larger group of women participants in the world of marketing.

I have reached deeply into my career experiences to offer an extra and very practical dimension to those factors affecting the woman marketer's life that are not found in standard texts. This book deals, among other factors, with politics and personalities; it is especially attentive to the benefits that women's high tuned, intuitive nature brings to the marketing process. That, in the broadest sense, is what marketing concerns itself with; and that is why among other reasons, the role of women and women's perspective with regard to the contemporary marketing function becomes worthy of exploration.

This book is dedicated to

Alfie,
who left before it was finished;

Jonharold,
who arrived in the middle of it;

and

Leslie and Amie,
who endured it all.

I

ELEMENTS OF MARKETING

1

Marketing: The Primary Business Strategy

MARKETING . . . WHAT IS IT?

If you were to put twelve marketing experts in a room and ask them to create a clear definition of marketing, they probably would die of old age before they could reach an agreement. To clear up any confusion, let me state at the beginning Maresca's marketing definition and philosophy: defining all the goals and objectives to be achieved, then using *whatever* tools or techniques it takes to reach them. The practice of marketing should be based 25 percent on marketing fundamentals and 75 percent on common sense; flexibility as to traditional rules, principles, or concepts; plus strong creative flair in implementation.

Marketing has proven its need again and again because without a sound strategy, without solid planning and implementation, a good idea will be just that—an idea that is never translated into a reality. Marketing can improve the fortunes of a company and, perhaps, civilization.

Civilization is helped because marketing is based on filling needs of the public—needs for better shelter, inexpensive foodstuffs, psychological gratifications, and so on. Needs will always exist. They have to be fulfilled, and the only way the fulfillment will come about is through planning and implementation, both of which are the major elements of strategy. And marketing is a strategy. It is intertwined into the business, economic, social, political, and virtually every other aspect of our daily lives. The marketer's role calls for identification and definition of needs, a comprehensive understanding of needs. She must understand needs, develop responses to those needs and wants, and persuade consumers to make a final marketing action.

Women are by nature more instinctive and more practical than men. Often operating against great odds, women have brought compassion, fashion, reality, and innovation to the marketing process. The result has been a more responsive mix of goods and services.

Woman's influence is felt in every category of consumer products, including such major expenditures as automobiles. It is woman's influence that has affected the style, the color, the comfort, and even the size of the product. The demographic emergence of woman as part of the work force has increased her purchasing influence both economically and preferentially. Today's woman is playing a much more outspoken role in the marketing process, not only as a consumer, but as a marketer helping companies choose the proper marketing direction and the proper products to meet consumer demands. Her potential contributions can amount to much more, however.

It is not the intention of this book to work out in great detail the fundamentals of the various aspects of the marketing process. These are available in many other places. I intend, rather, to take a few leaves from the pages of my experience and bring a broader, more down-to-earth point of view to the woman who is interested in her future and her influence in the marketing spectrum.

If you enter the field of marketing as a career, there is a fundamental truth that you should remember, for it will never change. Successful marketing is the cumulative effort of multiple factors. There is never a simple, single factor or action that will guarantee success. You must learn to look for and learn about all aspects of the marketing situation. Innumerable elements fall under the marketing umbrella, but what we are going to review are a number of primary elements which, when used in an interrelating manner, will give you marketing success.

Needs + Product/Service

The first step you must take is to identify the need or needs that you will fulfill. Although I might sound redundant on the principle of filling a need, this is a primary element of marketing. Let's look briefly at some of the products, services, and concepts around us that are successful. Think for a moment of how they fulfill a need that improves one's life-style, health, productivity, income, and much more.

Portable hair dryers, microwave ovens, chain saws, photocopiers, electric typewriters, electronic calculators, video tape recorders, car rental companies, fast food chains—the list goes on and on. Look at these and you can start to visualize the importance of marketing in filling a need. Many of these marketers guaranteed themselves a greater chance of success by carving out a niche that positioned their product or service differently than that of the competition, usually offering additional genuine benefits to the ultimate user of that product or service. The area of product/service is one we will come back to many times within this book. Basically, you want to remember that what you offer the public must fulfill a need. Next comes the identification of needs that need fulfilling. This brings us into the area of market research.

Market Research

Market research is a marketing element whose function is important to all aspects of the marketing mix. To many, market research has an aura of mystique surrounding it. In actuality, market research is a systematic and objective search for and analysis of information relevant to identifying and solving any marketing problem . . . or opportunity. Market research is considered an invaluable tool because of its unique ability to reduce the subjectivity of marketing judgments by supplying ascertainable and quantifiable facts. Marketing research makes two major contributions to a company. First, it helps the management of that company to recognize and set proper priorities as well as taking advantage of profitable opportunities such as new products, new channels of distribution, and the like. Second, marketing research allows a firm to identify problems. The research lets you know whether or not goals are being met and helps you to develop alternative solutions to problems and to verify information on which those decisions must be based. In short, market research increases one's ability to draw meaningful conclusions and make decisions in alternative marketing approaches; it will also give you some idea of the risks and consequences associated with alternative strategies and plans. The value of this specific marketing intelligence must be determined in terms of the risks involved in making marketing decisions, including the degree of uncertainty, investments required, and the potential profits at stake.

As an example, some years ago a major manufacturer of toiletries was about to make a judgment with respect to a repositioning of its leading, yet floundering, bath oil brand. Product research conducted in the form of focus sessions with both user and nonuser groups corroborated judgments about a psychological reward area as the best avenue for exploitation and share turnaround. Research identified the consumer benefit area, and it was then only a short step to relate such sought-after consumer rewards to prospective customers.

Another example is the case of a manufacturer with a home furnishings product that had been extremely successful in various parts of the Middle East. Senior management of the company was convinced that it would have equal success in the United States and were ready to plunk down $250,000 to promote the product to the consumer and the trade. They were convinced to spend a small percentage of that figure on research to find out whether or not the market really existed for this product. This research showed that the product, although popular in the Middle East, would not have had a successful reception here in the United States due to difference in life-style and perspective of value. This enabled the company to save a large sum of time and money, which would have been lost had the research not been done, as well as prevent extreme embarrassment to a firm, which has a high reputation within its industry.

Simply stated, marketing research will help you identify the opportunities and reduce the risks. Homework properly done on research will lead you to the next step—pricing.

Pricing

Pricing is the optimum level of dollar return you can secure for your product or service given your financial commitment within the framework of a competitive environment. Pricing is definitely a numbers game, especially if the best or right price has not yet been established within your industry. Generally, costs determine the basis for price, while demand and competition determine a flexible ceiling price. The pricing function unfortunately is not an automatic or impersonal process, but one of the more complicated marketing functions.

Pricing covers a multitude of factors, including primary costs, overhead, and profit. A basic pricing law states, "The higher the price of a product or service, the fewer total units will be purchased; the lower the price, the more units will be purchased." This law is not written in concrete and has had many successful exceptions. Look in the area of fashion. The designers' names found on higher-priced clothing, cosmetics, and so on did not reduce the number of units purchased. These names substantially increased purchases, plus the items were sold at a higher profit margin. There are many factors affecting the pricing area; obviously there's a high, middle, and low range for most product or service categories. You will want to locate your ideal price within one of these areas based on the research you have done regarding the potential size of the market, the competition, your operating costs, and your financial goals. Because the market of the eighties (and probably of the nineties as well) is highly fragmented, you should be able to test your product or service in various parts of the country at different price levels in order to get a feel for what will reap your largest return. Testing is one of the fundamentals of a good marketer, who utilizes this when the time and opportunity is appropriate, but never falls into the trap of relying solely on testing in order to make an appropriate marketing decision. You will never get away from the need to make decisions based on your own gut feeling, which we hope will be supported by years of experience and reinforced by the marketing intelligence data you have gathered.

Now that you have created a product/service that has been researched and properly priced, you must concentrate on distribution channels.

Distribution Channels

The word *channel* encompasses the sales force, agents, distributors, and retailers that are necessary for your product or service to reach the end user, the consumer. Keep in mind that in an industrial-based corporation, not all of those categories are necessary. Remember, some goods are sold directly to the end users, while others pass through middlemen before reaching their final buyers. What you as a marketer must concern yourself with is utilizing correct channels that have good access to the markets you wish to reach. This access is important because channels of distribution accomplish two primary functions: First, they transfer ownership of goods; and second, they physically move goods from the facilities of the manufacturer to those of the purchaser. Distribution channels also fulfill many other secondary but very important functions such as warehousing of products, transport and delivery of products, sharing in financial and time investments required, reducing the number of orders a buyer has to place, helping to establish a pricing for products, providing marketing communications and promotional services, as well as granting credit to buyers. It is important for you to remember that generally speaking, profit margins for the provider of goods or services are generally in direct proportion to the number of hands the item must pass through prior to its ultimate sale.

As an astute marketing executive you should examine all the alternatives open to you; select the types of distribution channels you feel are best suited for your needs; and select the specific sales force, agents, and distributors to help you flow your product or service through those distribution channels. Back those distribution channels up with thorough consumer marketing communications, such as . . .

Advertising

Advertising, as far as the consumer is concerned, is the most visual aspect of the communications segment of the overall marketing mix. It is your *paid* communications tool to get your message across through the media you choose—magazine, radio, television, direct mail, and so on. The specific intent is to influence consumers to purchase your product or service or otherwise react in a manner *you* desire. Do not lose sight of the fact that advertising does not make sales. It is not designed to do so, but rather to create a better atmosphere in which sales can be made. We go back to the cumulative effect of marketing. We have talked about development of the product, market research, pricing, and distribution, and now we're getting into the more visual marketing communications tools—but it is all of these together that will give you the success you are looking for, not any one of them alone. Advertising makes the salesperson's job easier. As an example of what advertising can do, let us relate the copy of a famous ad of McGraw-Hill's regarding why you should advertise. Visualize a grumpy-looking, hard-boiled buyer leaning forward and asking a poor unfortunate salesman in front of him the following: "I don't know who you are. I don't know your company. I don't know your company's product. I don't know what your company stands for. I don't know your company's customers. I don't know your company's record. I don't know your company's reputation. Now what was it you wanted to sell me?" Obviously, advertising helps your salespeople avoid such embarrassing questions, thus allowing them to immediately get to their main purpose of selling themselves, their company, and the company's product line and advertised product. There are many varied forms of advertising in existence, and new ones being developed each year. The degree to which you invest in advertising is dependent upon what it is you wish to offer the public and what is the size of the public you wish to offer it to.

If you were a manufacturer of a high-priced, large industrial machinery unit for which there may only be a handful of firms as potential buyers, you may not need to advertise at all. If your market is not so highly segmented and you have substantial competition for consumers' attention in your product category, then advertising is probably a necessity. Advertising is also your most effective tool for positioning the image of your product in the consumer's mind (think of the way McDonald's has given their restaurants a family-oriented image through very effective advertising). As your skill as a marketer increases, you will learn where to utilize advertising, the type to utilize, and when it is best to put heavy emphasis on advertising. The best example I can give of the latter aspect is that when we get into a recessionary period, one of the first things many companies do is to cut back their advertising expenditures. In reality, it is the area of advertising and other marketing communications tools that marketers should be expanding so that they will maintain their present share of the market, but increase it while their competitors cut back on their effort! A cutback results in less product and brand awareness and risks a drop in sales activity.

In addition to advertising, there is an equally important communications element in the marketing mix that is receiving substantially increased recognition . . .

Sales Promotion

There are those activities outside of advertising and public relations that stimulate consumer and retailer alike. They encompass couponing, premiums, point of sale, contests, sweepstakes, sampling, demonstrations, special events, audiovisual, and collateral material (manuals, product flyers, price sheets, catalogs, and brochures). According to many marketing experts, sales promotion is growing at twice the rate of advertising in amount of expenditure, although perhaps not in the level of sophistication. Sales promotion tools are designed to be measurable, to stimulate interest and response, and preferably to gain acceptance from a desired audience of your product or service. Sales promotion dollars, which now number into the billions, are spent not only on motivating customers and prospects, but are also used to motivate and assist management in the area of sales, employee productivity, distributor cooperation, and so forth.

In most marketing situations, advertising provides the *push* and sales promotion the *pull* to get the consumer to purchase the product or service you will be offering. Sales promotion is significantly more cost-efficient than advertising; it is obviously an invaluable force in the marketing process. Its emphasis on incentive activities such as couponing, sampling, contests, and the other areas we have discussed gives an extra dimension to the dynamism of the marketing process.

As with any successful formula, one additional ingredient can make a big difference. Advertising and sales promotion are very effective in the marketing process, but are substantially more result oriented when combined with a credibility factor developed by public relations.

Public Relations

Public relations is a builder of goodwill. There are many "publics" a company has to be concerned about: customers, retailers, wholesalers, employees, suppliers, government, the general community. Public relations consists of those activities that generate unpaid media exposure, creating credibility, excitement, and desirability for a product or service. Public relations activities serve as the hidden persuader in the marketing mix. They carry the force of truth precisely because they are not perceived by the consumer to be as commercial as other activities. I once heard a leading public relations executive explain at a seminar that approximately 87 percent of what you read in the newspaper has been put there by a public relations source. Public relations is equated with credibility; it can be accomplished in a variety of ways. If, for instance, you were about to introduce a new brand of dog food, a typical approach might be to issue a press release on the product and write it up for insertion in an important trade publication such as *Supermarket News*. This has the effect of telling key readers of that publication (buyers, store managers, and other management) that a distribution of sell-in effort for your product is under way. In this case public relations activities interrelate directly with the distribution component as well as the other marketing communications components. They generate product awareness and complement the distribution function at the sell-in stage.

Good public relations takes many forms in addition to the standard press release approach. It can take the form of mailings, an annual report, a special event, employee communications programs, open houses, plant tours, utilizing company speakers at local Rotary, company honors, and trade meetings, and more. Public relations is a very complex tool with a tremendous psychological bent to it. It is my recommendation that you obtain as many books as you can on this subject and look for opportunities to listen to proponents of public relations wherever they may speak. One aspect of public relations you should never lose sight of refers back to an area discussed earlier in this chapter, that of service. The people within your organization who have contact with the public at all levels are a source of positive or negative public relations reaction. It is recommended that firms institute a training program for all employees who might at some time project your firm's image to the public. This will assure the most positive image possible for your company, product, or service.

Suffice it to say that these basic interrelationships, when weighed one against the other and viewed from the point of view of what your competitor may be doing in the marketplace, are in reality your jumping-off point for the development of a marketing strategy. Ask lots of questions, both of yourself and of others. That's important. You'll scratch your head, choose one path over the other, weigh this factor and that, test the practicality of your evaluations against what you know you have in the bank, discard and start all over again. This is all part of the marketing game.

MARKETING REQUIRES TEAMWORK

As Theodore Levitt says:
Marketing is concerned with all the exhilarating big things and all the troublesome little things that must be done in every nook and cranny of the entire organization in order to achieve the corporate purpose of attracting and holding customers. This means that marketing is a consolidating view of the entire business process.

Marketing, like other schools of thought, has its group of supporters and those who feel its disciplines are not for them. Whether your ultimate goal is employment in a corporate structure or someday going into business for yourself, it is wise to remember that including marketing as a factor in your business strategy is a decision that will have an effect on all others in that business enterprise. It is therefore essential that all parties be brought into the fold. If you cannot make believers of them, at the very least, enlist their grudging cooperation. A spirit of teamwork and a proper psychological atmosphere which enforces the marketing philosophy are the keys to successful motivation. This encompasses all those business activities ancillary to the main thrust which at one point or another will come into contact with the marketing group. Manufacturing, finance, sales, administration, research, and development are a few that come to mind.

THE FORCE OF TRADITION

Why does the marketing-oriented company find itself too often in the role of having to convert the skeptics? It is tradition (which sometimes indicates a rut) that gets in the way. The natural evolution of corporate ways of doing business has for years been influenced by the energies of those who came first. If one manufactured, the focus of all gospel fixed its gaze on the machine. Production, that's what counted. Then the traditions of the peddler, the hawker of wares, took over. Widespread and inexpensive transportation allowed the traveling salesman to steal the limelight in the corporate hierarchy. The man who was out there on the firing line justifiably claimed a position of leadership; after all, he did have his finger on the pulse of what sells. The logical next step in the extension of corporate philosophy called for a mind that could both comprehend the need for these various functions and in turn lead those who were leading each of the individual segments. His or her ability has developed into the broader vision and management skill which we define as marketing. Standing back from the various parts, it should be the marketing manager who can see all the trees in the forest and how they can be interrelated.

MARKETING UNLIMITED

I am often asked if the broad reach of the marketing function can be used effectively in the different career fields that women contemplate. The answer is yes. It is always usable, and you are well advised to use it. Be it the producing of consumer products or the retail, service, and industrial business areas, all lend themselves ideally to the practice of marketing. Viewed in their individual perspectives, each of the following business areas offers great promise of marketing application.

The Retailing Business

Department stores, boutiques, drugstores, mass merchandise centers, supermarkets—these are what we call those sometimes beautiful, sometimes garish emporiums of goods that dot the American landscape. In order for the doors to open each day and the multitudes to march forward to trade for those things that nourish, beautify, cover, protect, educate, inform, and otherwise enhance our lives requires a number of marketing efforts before the cash register will ring. Someone, for example, has chosen to affix a certain character to the store. What will it be? What type of merchandise will it offer? At what price, and where will it be located? Bloomingdale's, a marvel of the retailing world, turned around years of declining profits by adopting a marketing stance that positioned its image as being a trend setter. Someone, a marketing man or woman, has been faced with the decision of where to locate the store. Are, for instance, the high rents associated with center city locations in line with the merchandise being offered? What is the public transportation capability? Will the thousands of shoppers required to make a profit be able to conveniently get to the goods? Yes, location—which in the retail sense is the distribution component of marketing—is critical. The 7-Eleven chain of convenience stores has become America's most successful retailer because of its expertise in matching retail access to shopper traffic patterns. Every act in the retail area must, of necessity, be concerned with one overriding factor—goods and customers. The right selection for the right people must be brought together in an environment that will make as easy as possible the exchange of something of value for another thing of value.

The Service Business

Service businesses are beginning to find ways to make their marketing efforts effective.

Banks, one of the oldest service institutions on the economic scene, have spent many years pondering the intricacies of how to let you have greater access to your money. Banks are paid a service charge for guarding, counting, and accounting for your hard-earned dollars. Each of the major commercial banks does essentially what its across-the-street competitor does. So why should a customer be motivated to choose one over the other? For years the answer has been in the area of personal relations. The reputations of banks have been handed down from father to daughter as good or bad places to do business. The marketing fever has hit these venerable segments of the service sector. Research has come up with the answer to gathering a larger piece of this business pie. Banks are convinced that they must give more of the same—more service—but of a different kind. So now the world of commercial banking is in the testing stages of a pivotal period in its business development. Will access to money via the check-cashing machine—open twenty-four hours a day, seven days a week, through fair weather or foul—tilt the curve of market share upward in favor of those institutions that are willing to invest millions to cement their product/customer transaction line? The point will be obvious. What marketing has ascertained is that banks are not in the money business. They are, as they have always been, in the service business. And it is the marketing of the service that is the product they must focus on if they are to grow and prosper.

The Consumer Product Business

Products for the consumer occupy the granddaddy spot in the marketing field. The reasons will be obvious. An example from the lives of consumers illustrates marketing and many of its components in action.

One day you wake up and the thing that hours before was the farthest thing from your mind is now in the medicine cabinet just next to the toothpaste. It has a shape, a color, a design, and even a name. Some astute marketer has succeeded in bringing you into his brand franchise. His brand is easily recognizable and therefore easily purchasable. It is different from others of its type.

Nowhere in the business world has the marketing philosophy been so successfully applied as it has in the consumer products area. Brands tell us why it is best to wash with them, smell of them, eat them, drink them. They accommodate to our color, life-style, spending habits, personal and aesthetic preferences. In some cases, they even define us. They can be positioned in such a way as to be status oriented, meaningful, practical, frivolous, or indulgent. This singular thing known as brand marketing or brand development is not easily reached. It is a well-studied, well-planned marketing avenue to offering that which will satisfy the consumer at his or her emotional, intellectual, and sensory levels. Research can probe minds to single out those voids in the product mix that might offer opportunity for new product development.

Manufacturing and research and development join in collaborative efforts to determine if available materials can be rearranged in such a way as to result in a meaningful product difference. Designers weigh and measure its size, shape, and color. How are we to get at the wonderful ingredients that lie inside the bottle? Will it fit on the supermarket shelf? Will it ease into that space next to the toothpaste in the medicine cabinet? Will it travel, pack in an attaché case, fit in a desk drawer or car glove compartment? Will the average consumer pay the extra seventeen cents per unit for the privilege of having it come foil-sealed in individual dispenser packs? How will she view this form of application in contrast to the cumbersome, large economy size she has been purchasing for the past three years? Should we offer her a free sample in the hopes that she will like it enough to pay for the next one? Agree shampoo delivered approximately fifty million samples in its introduction and the brand is doing well. And in what programs will the television commercial be most effective? To what age group? To what income level? As against what editorial background or format? Is it news that makes the viewer most receptive to commercials? Denture manufacturers such as Warner Lambert believe such programs add to the credibility of their products' claims. Or should we look to the intimacy of a daytime soap opera? Are we better off reaching one million people all at once or the same million over a period of time? Polaroid took the former route with its Polarvision and the results have been poor. And what kind of stores do we put this brand in? Big ones, little ones, a few or many? And where in the store? Up front, in a special section, in a special display, hanging from a hook, near the cash register, with or without a display sign? Ferrero USA built a number-one position in the mint business because it designed a gravity-feed display that could fit into the small space available at a supermarket check-out counter.

Then once we've found that special blend of marketing ingredients that will get this brand into our lives, how will we react to it over a period of time? Will we take the time to answer the short questionnaire that the manufacturer has enclosed in the package? Will we satisfied users tell our friends about it, thereby providing the manufacturer with the hardest-to-come-by, cheapest, and most valuable advertising—word of mouth? I'm reminded of St. Laurent's Opium perfume. The mystery and connotation of the name moved rapidly from woman to woman. All of these things are part of the behind-the-scenes marketing activities that are developed and implemented by the women and men in the consumer products marketing area. Here is one of the most sophisticated business operations ever developed. And the market test in small model cities? The test, designed to get the bugs out of the campaign, reduces the financial risk. Are we ever really aware that tests are being conducted, perhaps in some of our very own cities and in other geographically dispersed cities throughout the country? Are we aware that these tests may well have national implications for this brand's future marketing? Most of us are not aware. But the aspiring marketer will of course be aware that in the big risk, big reward consumer-goods marketplace, to the diligent marketer, the rewards of product acceptance can be significant.

The Industrial Business

The world of industrial products, heavy manufacturing, and high technology has in the past shown limited use of the marketer's skills. Industrialists have done business in a traditional manner for years, but the decade of the eighties is tossing tradition out the window at a rapid rate. A new mental environment is required due to changes in the economy, in business, and in the aggressiveness of competitors, especially those from other nations. Marketing will play a major role in the growth of the industrial sector.

Trade advertising exhibits, sales meetings, and direct mail have been the traditional mainstays of this segment of business. Now you will be seeing the utilization of electronic video techniques in cable TV, sales meetings, and pronouncements via satellite video networks—all new tools and techniques in communicating on a mass as well as an individualized basis. Sales promotion will be playing a bigger role. Techniques used in the consumer area are being tried for the first time in the industrial sector—rebates, coupons, premiums, sweepstakes, and so on.

Women have been playing an ever-increasing role in the sales area of the industrial sector; that experience will, by need of the industry, open the door to marketing management to those who have shown an inclination for this area of specialization. The industrial marketplace offers women superb opportunities.

2

New Product Development

The marketer who would bring to her work a fully developed business perspective will no doubt find that a comprehensive knowledge of new product development is helpful. There are those factors that are particularly pertinent to the American economic system which give birth to the new product development emphasis. In addition, there are the techniques for implementing the new product drive which can be utilized in most areas in the consumer goods, industrial, and service sectors of the marketplace.

ONCE UPON A TIME AMERICA DISCOVERED THE CONSUMER. Nowhere in the spectrum of economic development has the stimulation of anticipation and institutionalization of the consumer been more finely honed than it has been in this country. We have, as a nation, a unique niche in the world economic order for our genius at extending the skills of the tinkerer in the direction known as new product development. Whether to build a better mousetrap or to bring products which in the real sense of the word are new to the marketplace, American marketers are extraordinary. The historical emphasis on that which is new is peculiar to America for the very same reasons our forefathers embraced when they first set out to this country. The spirit of the adventurer, which lay at the heart of the early pioneers, was successively regenerated in each new wave of immigration. America has always held out the prospect of the new and the uncharted.

POST-WORLD WAR II NEW PRODUCT IMPETUS.   As the country settled back in the peaceful mold for which so many had sacrificed so much, Americans got down to the business of conspicuous consumption. So many years of doing with less or doing without left an enormous reserve of pent-up demand. American marketing genius was ready for the task. Utilizing technology sometimes developed by the government, the turn to peacetime uses developed into a product explosion that has seen no equal—and it all happened in three short decades. To provide better-tasting food and more leisure time in which to enjoy it, the microwave oven was invented. To satisfy the demands of liberated life-styles, the health-care industries gave us the birth control pill. To bring the human touch of photography within the technological reach of all Americans, the Polaroid Land Camera was invented. It was appropriate for an age that demanded instant gratification at almost every turn—the instant camera. Frozen foods solved the problems of crop shortage, shopping-time problems, and better-balanced diets. The pocket calculator, which makes mathematicians out of even the minimally educated, has extended itself into the electronic game. Today a consumer can play chess electronically, plot the movement of particular astrological signs and phenomena if they are so inclined, or even select a mate through the wonders of computer matching. Skills of rocket scientists have been utilized by the managerial genius of America's aerospace industry to make jumbo jet travel so all-pervasive that the railroad system of the country is no longer the viable means of long-distance transportation it once was. Each of these products has been successful because the need was there and the marketing mechanism was found which could develop these needs into paying business propositions.

Everybody Loves a New Product

The economic soundness of new product development cannot be challenged. Products, like people, have life cycles. For a variety of different reasons, they will inevitably find their sales curves peaking—and then will begin the descent downward. Since business cannot afford a static sales curve, it must constantly be on the lookout for new ways to generate sales. The two avenues available to accomplish this are the finding of new markets for existing products and the development of new products to satisfy newly designated market needs. The new product approach first and foremost is concerned with the needs and desires of consumers. It is one process that all can easily relate to. Product needs are impacted by psychological values, thus making the need for a constant flow of new products a more emphatic one. The area of packaged goods, for example, is one where the changing psychological attitudes of the broad range of consumer opinion found in America is more apparent.

STEP ONE: DEVELOPING THE IDEA.   Though ideas can and do come from any source, it is most often the case that they blossom best when the atmosphere is right. The environment must be open, receptive, nurturing, and motivating. Smart management recognizes the desirability of ideas and fosters the dynamics, formal or informal, that will bring them to the surface.

Obviously, to find one good idea you need to generate a large number to choose from. A systematic approach to idea development will help, such as:

1.   Get your sales staff and/or market research department to aid you in better understanding your customers' needs, purchasing habits, motives, and product usage patterns; problems encountered; and desirable product characteristics. This could lead to product improvement and new product development.

2.   Investigate new and standard technologies and the possibility of combining them.

3.   Think of specific customer groups and market segments for a new product search.

4.   Encourage all internal sources to suggest ideas for new products or product improvements.

5.   Utilize a formal suggestion box system. Make it easy for people to suggest by using a form that stimulates thought. Be sure to give recognition and awards for adopted ideas.

6.   Organize brainstorming sessions. Encourage freewheeling thinking, while eliminating criticism of any idea until all have had time to think it over.

7.   Don't be afraid to ask your customers what they might like to see in a new product.

Here are eight words that might aid in generating new ideas:[*]

- *Adapt?* What else is this like? What other ideas does this suggest? Does the past offer a parallel? What could I copy? Whom could I emulate?
- *Modify?* New twist? Changing meaning, color, motion, sound, odor, form, shape? Other changes?
- *Magnify?* What to add? More time? Greater frequency? Stronger? Higher? Longer? Thicker? Extra value? Plus ingredient? Duplicate? Multiply? Exaggerate?
- *Minify?* What to subtract? Smaller? Condensed? Miniature? Lower? Shorter? Lighter? Omit? Streamline? Split up? Understate?

[*]Source: Alex F. Osborn, *Applied Imagination*, Charles Scribner & Sons.

- *Substitute?* Who else instead? What else instead? Other ingredient? Other material? Other process? Other power? Other place? Other approach? Other tone of voice?
- *Rearrange?* Interchange components? Other pattern? Other layout? Other sequence? Transpose cause and effect? Change pace? Change schedule?
- *Reverse?* Transpose positive and negative? How about opposites? Turn it backward? Turn it upside down? Reverse roles? Change shoes? Turn tables? Turn other cheek?
- *Combine?* How about a blend, an alloy, an assortment, an ensemble? Combine units? Combine purposes? Combine appeals? Combine ideas?

STEP TWO: IDEA EVALUATION/MARKET RESEARCH.   There is usually considerable judgmental agreement as to the pertinency of the idea; some assurance is needed that the technology, equipment, and components exist for manufacturing the product. Initial cost estimates are done which seek to place the financial parameters of the investment which will be required, plus a hard look at purchase-price structure and how it relates to the prospective customer. At this stage a probe of customer attitudes is often taken, especially for consumer products. Such research is a complex and sophisticated process often involving actual usage of prototype products to solicit consumer reaction, as well as an in-depth exploration of all the dynamics that make up the consuming segment of any one marketplace. For example, the marketers who initially conceived using the microwave oven for home use would have been well advised to probe prospective consumers along the following lines:

Areas of Interest

Demographics: The basics would include age, sex, occupation, income, education, city, and size of family and residence.

Statistical: Would seek to probe eating and cooking habits. The number of working women, single people, and so on.

Motivating Factors: Would probe current life-style habits, utilization of time, importance of hobbies and other interests, especially outside the home.

Emotional Factors: Would proble likes and dislikes having to do with cooking.

Distribution System: Would probe the entire area of how this product would be received by the dealer network, as well as its influence and importance.

This brief example highlights probable areas of interest and concern to the marketer and is intended as an outline for what might ultimately become a questionnaire incorporated into an actual consumer survey.

MICROWAVE QUESTIONNAIRE

Please tell us: A) frequency with which you cook meals (per week):

        1–2 _____ 3–4 _____ 5–6 _____ Over 6 _____

    B) approximate number of people at each meal:

breakfast	_____	1–2	3–4	5–6	6+
lunch	_____	1–2	3–4	5–6	6+
dinner	_____	1–2	3–4	5–6	6+

    C) foods most frequently cooked and served:
       (number list in order of most popular)

        steak   chicken
        lamb   turkey
        roast beef   ham

    D) what type of range/oven do you now own?

        gas _____ electric _____

Respondent is: male _____ female _____

    age bracket:

    19–25 _____ 25–40 _____ 40–55 _____ 55–70 _____

    employed:

    _____ homemaker: _____ student: _____

    household income:

    under $15K __ $20–40K __ Over $40K __

It is the first step in the professional process which seeks to make the rule of realism mix with the rules of innovation. The answers, in the case of the microwave manufacturers, were positive. This astute marketer had determined that a need in the marketplace existed.

You might consider seven questions which in general are good guidelines in the initial screening process of new product development.

1. Will it do anything for the customer?
2. Will it really fill a need or desire? How?
3. Can the customer specifically save time, labor, materials, facilities, or money? How?
4. Will it make the customer's work easier, more convenient, more pleasurable? How?
5. How do these ideas compare with existing products?

6. Is the product concept compatible with your company's objectives?
7. Is the timing in the marketplace right?

The Concept Test

Concept testing is utilized by many marketers as a second step in the new product development process. Concepts (verbalized or written ideas) that describe the product or service under consideration are exposed to groups of likely users for their reaction. There may be several versions of the same basic idea offered, and the research technique seeks to get an intention-to-purchase level and a relative rating of one preferred concept as opposed to the others. The concept test has its prime utility in determining new product ideas that are ripe for exploitation by measuring those that rate at the high end of the scale against those that fall low down on the intention-to-purchase ladder.

Interpreting the Research

As marketers sift through the findings of their research investment, a refined product is most usually the result. It may come in the form of a change in package color, trade profit margins, the quality offered, the depth of the line (for example, must a new cosmetic really come in fifteen different shades or will seven basically do?), or the name of the product (Exxon worked through over five thousand computer-generated letter configurations before finally arriving at that new designation for the giant oil company). Or the product concept may be altered to accommodate the market needs of consumers that are determined by the user's sex. Scott's decorated toilet tissue is a direct response to a research-derived fact. Women had taken to viewing the bathroom as a reflection of their life-styles. It was to be decorated and treated like all other rooms in the house, which had traditionally been spruced up and put on display.

APPRAISAL DECISIONS AND MARKET POTENTIAL.   Prior to the testing of a new product in a limited (as to dollars) environment, and to further reduce the risk of the product failure, certain basic business decisions have to be made. The likelihood of purchase by a large enough group of consumers must be measured. Research findings on sample groups large enough for accurate statistical projections can be used for this purpose. But you should consider the evaluation of seven factors:

1. Market size—potential volume.
2. Market share—realistic view of your potential percentage of business.

3. Location—how important? In retail sales? In distribution?
4. Diversity potential—is it needed in more than one area?
5. How strong is the growth pattern of the industry?
6. How will business react in a recession?
7. Will this give you a foothold in a new field?

Marketability

Will the price at which you sell the new product be competitive, or will the unique difference make a premium price possible? That is just one of many questions that have to be answered. Others to think about are: Do you have enough qualified sales people? Are the existing distribution channels suitable? Is the product easy to promote? What is the potential of customer loyalty? Of government or ecological opposition? What about life cycle?

LIFE CYCLE.   Will this be an item with an extended life cycle in the marketplace? Marketers will think differently about fashion-oriented, short-life products than they will about more basic and fundamental advances. There is a certain solid feeling that the microwave oven brings to the savvy manufacturer. He will be more likely to invest large sums of money in a product like this which so clearly outdistances others.

FEASIBILITY.   How practical are the technical aspects of the product? How strong is your technical capability? Production capacity? What is the situation regarding materials availability? Regarding service support? Regarding warehousing space?

ECONOMICS.   What is your development cost? What is the tooling and manufacturing cost? What do you expect as a return on investment? Do you have sufficient capital available? How long a payback period is needed? What will be your break-even point? These are a few factors that must be taken into account to determine the success potential of a new product.

LEGAL ASPECTS.   Considerable advantage accrues to that marketer who can protect the new product with a patent. The competitive nature of the American marketplace makes it mandatory to protect a product advantage as best one can. So you must thoroughly investigate patentability and trademark and copyright protection, especially in the advertising area. Don't forget that "Big Brother" (the government) is always looking over your shoulder, so you must view legislative action as an area of concern. Last, but extremely important, is the area of product warranty. In new product development, the legal factors play as important a role as all other factors, if not more so. Do your homework well. It will pay.

Test Marketing

This is a critical phase for the new product development team. Test markets limit financial risk, provide further refinement of the product concept, and quantify sales and cost forecasting. The test market is the final stage before the marketer moves his or her new concept against the broader and more-expensive-to-reach national base of prospect customers. The wise marketer realizes that though it may seem to take endless time, the new product test-marketing process can be the best safeguard against unnecessary market losses.

Taking the Pulse
of the New Product

One of the critical problems marketers of new products will encounter is the ability to properly read results of new product testing when the laboratory of the test market is being utilized. There are usually a host of barometers in addition to actual sales statistics which have to be taken into account. The most difficult task is knowing how much time to allow for the process to unwind—when to call it a success or failure is as critical a judgment as the marketer will make. Data is not always conclusive: Sometimes certain information—for example, reports of participating stores' warehouse withdrawal—may be in conflict with store audit information, which measures what the consumer is doing. Judging the time factor can be made easier if one looks at the curve of activity/ development of new product sales in the marketplace. Most marketers agree that there are distinct stages: introduction, which is usually slow in ascendency; growth, which can be characterized as a balloon effect; maturity, a prolonged period of flattening out of the sales curve; and finally, the downward trend of the sales curve.

WHO WILL SUPPORT YOUR EFFORTS?   There are two distinct groups whose acceptance and support of the new product is vital. The first is that group within the marketers' own organization who will decide that a certain product merits full support. If the decision is yes, then a new product, which should be advertised and promoted heavily, will receive the support it needs to give it a chance to become a major brand. Negative response will inevitably doom it to failure or, at the very least, give it a less realistic chance in the marketplace. The marketer who has a true product advance in a category that is heavily promoted must minimally do something to raise the public's awareness level of the product to a parity level with that of its competitors if it is to make a dent. The second group of gatekeepers are those persons and industries, allied or tangential to the new product, whose own interests are directly related to the product. For example, the supermarket which seeks to attract young mothers as a key consumer purchasing group will cooperate closely with the marketer whose new baby product can be featured in a newly designed section of the supermarket that will feature a full range of baby products, from baby foods to disposable diapers. Reading the merchandising trends of a key class of retail trade is an activity marketers must be attuned to.

Altering a Product's Life-style

Senior marketers are aware that nothing is quite so certain as the continuing change they will encounter in the marketplace. The process of repositioning products whose life cycle has declined for the purpose of giving them new life is a technique marketers must be aware of. In the days of cheap energy, for example, the newly introduced Volkswagen was sold on its merits as an inexpensive second car. It was thought of as being perfect for short trips only. Today's repositioning, which features gas economy, the comfort of the ride, and the enlarged interior, has given it a new boost in the marketplace. In today's energy-impacted economy, the Volkswagen is not only a family's first car, it is often the only car.

Times have changed, and marketers have been quick to grasp the implications of such change. The marketers of expensive cigarette lighters had been hesitant to cannibalize and trade down their line of lighters in the face of low-priced competitors. Thus the disposable Bic captured a portion of that business which has altered as a result of a change in the perception of the cigarette lighter in the eyes of the consumer. No longer viewed as a gift or a piece of jewelry, the lighter has been relegated to the ranks of the disposable. To survive—if it is not already too late—the other high-ticket manufacturers will also have to reposition. The underwear field provides another example. Thermal underwear, long viewed as an unseen, warmth-providing garment for persons whose work took them outside during frigid weather, has been redesigned as fashion wear. Bright colored thermal shirts and bottoms are now standard equipment for those skiers, joggers, snowmobile buffs, and skaters whose desire for warmth and fashion have created an entirely new market.

Notwithstanding the perils of inflation and the perils of investment by marketers in new product development, one thing seems pretty certain. Ingenious marketers will continue to search for the new and innovative product or service. American consumers, severely affected by the cost of living index, will continue to respond to the product or service that is pertinent to their needs, captures their imaginations, and offers a credible alternative choice to that which they may already be using.

3

Sales Promotion: The Measurable Marketing Tool

Sales promotion encompasses all those activities outside of advertising and public relations, at both the trade and consumer levels, that are utilized to elevate the possibility of sales. It is the actionable and accountable ingredient in a synergistic mix of marketing activities which includes advertising. Together they create an awareness of a product or service; and then a *push* from the sales promotion activity causes the net effect, completing the sale.

A Renaissance in Marketing Technique

The emergence of sales promotion as a major force in the marketing mix occurred as a result of a fundamental shift in the marketing world. The emphasis on long-term investment and growth principles has put a major importance on the more expedient short-term need for instant activity and results. Sales promotion, a more sales-oriented, action-oriented marketing tool, is ideally suited to this. There are certain characteristics of sales promotion that are fueling the growth of this communication element in the marketing mix.

Measurability

Measurability of well-executed sales promotion efforts has brought forth results that have generated increased willingness of senior management to view promotion in its proper perspective as a marketing function.

Legitimacy

Sales promotion is fully recognized as an effective and legitimate marketing enterprise. The success of rebate programs, couponing, sampling, premium offers, and much more have hastened the acceptance of this marketing technique so that sales promotion expenditures now far exceed advertising expenditures.

Executive Upgrading

As a result of the broad recognition of the economic soundness of the sales promotion activity, companies have invested in better-qualified and better-trained specialists in the sales promotion area to do the job. Higher-caliber management is responsible for higher-caliber results. The emphasis on immediate return to the bottom line and the focus of senior management's eyes on the product/brand manager who can deliver growth and profits for his brands has hastened the growth of sales promotion activity.

Let's briefly review some of the more prevalent promotion techniques in use today.

PREMIUMS

Self-Liquidator

The offering manufacturer intends to only recoup their costs of the premium plus the administrative costs involved in fulfilling the offer. For example, when Kellogg's offers the consumer a set of decorated water goblets worth $10.00 for $3.95 plus two proofs of purchase from cornflakes boxes, they have given the consumer a real value to take advantage of. The consumer who provides proofs of purchase with a premium offer has been motivated to pick one brand over another, plus make repeat purchases. In this case, the premium offer was being used to stimulate product movement in the supermarket.

On-Pack

These premiums are so named because the free bonus product is packed right with the item, which is available for normal purchase. Special packing is designed to house the bonus item, often in such a manner as to make it visible. Such premiums usually have a significant effect on the eye of the shopper as he or she moves down a supermarket aisle; they are often used as a short-term stimulus to sales. A Bic pen taped to a bottle of household cleaner is an example of an on-pack premium.

In-Pack

These are usually continuing giveaways such as games, toys, place mats, and the like, packaged in boxes of cereal or other food products. Often the manufacturers' intent is to cement brand loyalty by setting up a collecting or ongoing premium connection which will persuade the user to make that particular brand and its premium a habit. Cracker Jacks has encouraged repeat sales for years using this method of premium.

Straight Giveaway

This incentive is quite popular with fast-food marketers such as Hardees, McDonald's, Burger King, Pizza Hut, and others. It is a free gift, usually advertised either in paid media or via store signage. Its purpose is simply to build traffic, to entice a prospect into the store. A purchase is not always required. It is utilized to set up a friendly atmosphere; in essence, it tells the consumer that the particular outlet is a good place to get a little bonus for visiting. Examples of the straight giveaway are the free balloons or comic books given to children, or the free glass given with a purchase of beverage.

Free Mail-in Offer

This is another collecting or save-up technique. It requires the accumulation of a certain specified number of labels which, when sent in, can be redeemed for free gifts. It is an interesting technique in that the slippage factor—those consumers who do not stay with the offer long enough to gather all the required labels—is significant. This technique affords the marketer a stimulus above and beyond his normal sales rate without his having to underwrite the full cost impact of redemption.

Dealer Loader

This is a primary sell-in technique to retailers when large amounts of display space are being sought by the marketer. In most cases the premium is directed to store personnel, who will be allowed to keep the gift for themselves. Gifts can either come packaged with the special display unit shipped directly to the retailer's home or be packed with the shipment itself.

ADVERTISING SPECIALTIES

The basic purpose of ad specialties is to enhance brand name awareness—that is, to keep the name of the product or service uppermost within the mind of the prospective customer. To be effective, the specialty should reflect the overall timing of the marketing program and carry with it a certain degree of real utility for the recipient. These are usually items given away free by the marketer. The basic difference between ad specialties and premiums is that the specialty carries the name or logo of the marketer prominently stamped upon the items, while the premium does not. In recent years, premiums of well-known marketers have begun to carry brand-name imprints as well. Remember, however, that while a premium can be given free, it requires action on the part of the consumer to receive the premium. Advertising specialties do not.

Advertising specialties encompass a wide variety of products, such as buttons with slogans or designs that catch the public's attention and act as a walking billboard (these are useful as identification at trade shows, sales meetings, etc.); calendars, ranging from the desk type for executives to the type retailers give out for home use; ceramic mugs; matchbooks; pens, pencils; shopping bags; balloons; and award plaques. The list is never-ending, encompassing thousands of items. Your source for these low-cost but highly effective sales promotion tools is your local member of the Specialty Advertising Association.

SWEEPSTAKES

This area of the sales promotion spectrum has received widespread attention, and for good reason. The key advantage of sweepstakes utilization is that the scope of the offer is usually so large, usually carries with it such tremendous prize value, that when properly conceived, the promotional piece carrying the incentive offer will most often command an impressive space allocation in the retail outlet, as it is also a traffic builder. Sweepstakes, which offer a chance to win a European vacation, automobile, or other big-ticket prizes (many of which are travel/vacation related) are an excellent sales promotion technique with a special cost-control benefit built in. Marketers utilizing them deal with fixed cost for the prize offered. Unlike the standard premium, there are few variables as to cost. There is also a fairly accurate response rate which can be determined for this type of offer. This further facilitates the decision-making process with respect to choosing one method of sales stimulus over another. In terms of payout to the marketers, sweepstakes are a fairly safe promotional investment.

DIRECT MAIL

For the most part these are efforts aimed at the consumer in which offers are made by mail. They are often done on either an occupant-of-building or domicile basis or through selected lists which distinguish between the various demographic profiles desired. To explain consumer mailings further is unnecessary for obvious reasons, as everyone at some time or other has found him- or herself the recipient of a charity request, merchandise catalog, book offer, and so forth, all of which use the mails to sell.

There is within this category a large portion of activity that is trade-directed, also. Usually it is mail of a nature that calls attention to a newly available product—a special deal that offers better-than-usual buying terms, information as to pricing, and the like. In this area, considerable attention is paid to the graphic look of the mailing piece, for in many circumstances it will be the backbone of a marketing effort. It serves to bridge the gap between the product's announcement, which may be heralded in important trade or business press advertising, and the arrival of the company's salesman for his call.

TRADE SHOWS/EXHIBITS

The practice of meeting one's customers at shows, exhibits, and conventions is deeply ingrained in the sales promotion mechanism of marketers worldwide. Such trade shows provide a market for the display of goods and services, utilizing the technique of one centralized location to display the lines of merchandise of all vendors who have a stake in any one industry. The prime utility of such shows is to serve as a central clearinghouse. Because of them, companies of all sizes are able to display their products to a broad audience, utilizing the effectiveness of large convention halls and heavy customer traffic to minimize their selling costs. Such gatherings employ a dazzling array of display techniques in order to showcase their wares. The trade show business is big business, often including a special journal printed specifically for such shows, with major advertising commitments by participating exhibitors.

PROMOTION/SPACE ADVERTISING

This is that area of media advertising devoted to the support of sales promotion incentives efforts. It is a category that has grown tremendously in the last years; it includes that portion of advertising devoted to the communication of certain consumer promotion techniques like the freestanding newspaper insert, which often contains a host of cents-off consumer coupons and is delivered to the home of the prospect.

PRINTING PRODUCTION

The preparation of elaborate brochures—including every conceivable form of printed piece, from the four-page flyer, which will stuff easily into a standard-size business envelope, to a thirty-two-page full color annual report, which may be mailed in quantities as high as 250,000—constitutes a significant investment in print production dollars for major marketers.

AUDIOVISUAL

The audiovisual presentation is fast becoming a standard, particularly for those industries in which a message of very specific dimensions and sequence must be adhered to. Everything from fairly simple 35mm slide shows to elaborate videotape or cassette presentations are utilized. Marketers are rapidly discovering that in many cases it is best to let the salesperson simply introduce him or herself, then let the film carry the salient selling message to the viewer.

POINT OF PURCHASE DISPLAY

The utilization of eye-catching displays to capture the attention of buyers is of considerable importance to certain industries. The liquor industry has for years relied heavily on elegant displays to capture market share. They are particularly discernible at high-consumption periods such as Christmas and New Year's. In the food field, the use of large corrugated set-up displays and other semipermanent units are a standard form of merchandising. The vast bulk of these display dollars are directed to the consumer, though in some cases displays are conceived for the purpose of conveying a corporate or special-interest message. The construction of panoramic displays requires considerable investment on the part of the participating industries.

BUSINESS MEETINGS

Business meetings, a trade-directed effort, take up a significant portion of the sales promotion budgets of large companies. Often they serve as a kickoff point for a major sales drive or other major marketing effort. Housed at a central location, often in a resort atmosphere, they are structured to allow for a mix of seminarlike activities and an important measure of freedom and relaxation for those attending.

MOTIVATING INCENTIVES

The proper management of the sales promotion function, as it interrelates with all the other ingredients available to the marketer, is dependent on those skills of the manager that focus on planning and coordinated execution. These short case histories of marketers considered to have employed the sales promotion function as part of their winning market strategy demonstrate the level of sophistication required for bringing together seemingly diverse techniques to achieve a market goal.

Imperial Sugar

Increasing the market share in a commodity category such as sugar is probably one of the most difficult tasks a marketer can address. There is, for all intents and purposes, little difference between products. Recognizing this, the marketers at the Dallas-based company sought to ally themselves with a parallel industry—home canning—in an effort directed toward increasing product usage by emphasizing tangential uses for a low-interest-product category. The strategy was well planned and brilliantly executed. Imperial marketing management sought to involve all elements (consumer and trade) in the marketing mix, in a broad coordinated effort. Seeking out the right partners, Imperial joined forces with a century-old home canning company, Ball. They centered their joint promotional drive on the *Ball Bluebook*, a home canning instructional manual, offering it to consumers at a considerable saving. The strategy of promoting home canning as a young-homemaker activity obviously involved the utilization of sugar—in this case, of course, the Imperial brand. Extensive promotion included store-located home canning displays near the produce section, a home economist tour of TV shows of special interest to women, plus extensive consumer advertising of the book offer. Added to this was an on-pack premium offer—7.5 million Imperial Sugar cartons carried the Imperial offer. The combined program contributed to a significant increase in the usage of sugar, and Imperial's share far outgained its competitors.

Weight Watchers

The marketing strategies of this company have always focused on two directions at the same time. In order to profitably operate this unique business, marketing management must continually seek to attract new users while at the same time offering incentives that will keep old users beyond a certain period of time. It is obvious that the profits of the company are directly related to the length of time of membership—it takes time to deliver on the promise of weight loss—and this retention objective is the most difficult of the two tasks to achieve. Coming off a formidable sales increase of 28 percent in 1978, attributable in good measure to a less stringent list of foods included in the Weight Watchers plan, the combined new member/old member retention drive seemed strong indeed. By utilizing a discounted new members' registration fee of four dollars tied to a commitment by these members to stay a minimum of five weeks, together with a free copy of the *Weight Watchers International Cookbook* to all members who stayed on the program for a minimum of ten weeks, the marketer's goals were achieved. The new-member enrollment rate increased by 59 percent, with 50 percent of those members staying with the plan for a full ten weeks. Of those remaining, 70 percent stayed the full cycle of ten weeks. Though the four-dollar discount was considered a calculated risk, its linkage with the cookbook offer more than offset any losses by virtue of its volume-producing effect on member retention for the longer course.

PLANNING
SALES PROMOTION PROGRAMS

The marketing manager of the future has a more complex set of skills to master than did her predecessor. With the explosion that has taken place in the sales promotion arena, major marketers are requiring that their senior personnel be as fully conversant with this aspect of the marketing function as they are with all the other ingredients.

Be aware of those steps most pertinent to the planning of your sales promotion efforts:

1. Define those markets you wish to be targets of your campaign.
2. Include all data on characteristics, desires, and needs of the target markets.
3. Identify the most appealing approaches to dealing with selected market segments.
4. Review nature of product, sales history, life-cycle stage, buying process, and competition's efforts.
5. Develop a cost and effectiveness rating on the various promotion tools available.
6. Develop an idea file from other companies' promotions.
7. Choose those techniques best suited for your target market and goal.
8. Tie the theme and message of your promotion to the needs of your audience.
9. When feasible, test!

Coordinate

All sales promotion efforts should be communicated to those key areas of the marketing structure, primarily sales and market planning and research.

Measure

The validity of market performance measurements must be questioned if the effect of sales promotion activities has not been taken into account. It is no longer a viable or intelligent position to attribute a broadened All Commodity Index of Distribution to the effects of pull-through advertising efforts only. Such devices as dealer loaders, cents-off couponing, the entire area of premiums and travel incentives, as well as special efforts directed at sell-in activities, must be weighed in making the evaluation.

Companies throughout the land recognize the importance of professionals managing a professional undertaking. Though coming of age may have been too long a process, the sales promotion specialist is an important member of today's marketing team. As advertising costs can be expected to continue their upward and less affordable spiral, more and more sophisticated companies will be looking toward the well-qualified and experienced sales promotion specialists to lead the push/pull efforts of coordinated sales promotion and advertising drives.

4

Personal Selling

Nowhere in the personal revolution that has freed women from debilitating stereotypes has the task of achievement been more difficult and more rewarding than in that last stronghold of male-only mentality, the salesforce position. Chapter 10 touches on the area of personal sales as one that might serve women well should they aspire to broader corporate involvement in a marketing position. The spoils of victory will and should most logically belong to that person who can make a contribution to the selling efforts of an organization. Sales are indeed what makes the marketing world go around.

> Salesmanship Consists Of Transferring A Conviction By A
> Seller To A Buyer—Paul Hoffman

No field has as many quotations, truisms, or clichés written about its activities than sales. Many of them can be extremely helpful to the beginner, as well as serving as worthwhile reminders to the experienced professional.

A cliché is a proven wisdom, so don't ignore it. "Nothing happens until someone sells something to somebody" is quite true. All of us are salespeople. Every day of our lives we are selling, if not a product or service, an idea. If not one on one, to many. Sales performance is the lifeblood of the business world and thus of the American economy.

It is my opinion that sales is a profession equivalent to that of medicine or law. The skilled salesperson is fabulous to see in action, as she must be multitalented, ranging from a psychiatrist to an actor. Sales is a field in which the emerging working woman is making a strong track record.

One On One

The resistance of male-dominated management to the utilization of females as sales personnel has never made sense and is rapidly disappearing. The problems confronting those managements who recognize the importance of their sales efforts are just too great. Practicality and reality have raised their heads, and management has bowed to common sense. Those persons who combine the rare qualities of personal courage, persistence, emotional maturity, persuasiveness, adaptability, and, above all, the need to achieve are just too valuable to judge on the basis of sex alone or to relegate to an administrative inside position. Sales are a costly undertaking; as such, they demand the best one-on-one talents available. The figures tell the story. The latest statistics regarding direct costs charged to sales budgets throughout corporate America exceeded the mind-boggling 100-billion-dollar level. So as to relate this expenditure to other major marketing activities, one need only be reminded that recently, expenditures for advertising were at the 24-billion-dollar level, and those for sales promotion somewhat exceeded the 30-billion-dollar mark.

Making It

The salesperson is involved, for all intents and purposes, in a linkage function. This is the same activity that in every sense of the word is at the heart of the marketing process. There have been innumerable studies seeking to define that personality and those traits that the most-likely-to-succeed sales personality will possess. Few of these studies have been more than moderately successful. The combination of talents and motivations required are evidently so diverse, and the process that focuses them on one woman rather than another so esoteric that they actually defy pigeonholing—and perhaps this is all to the good. Formula approaches as such do not seem to suit what we have come to describe as the sales type. There is drama involved. Selling is theater. The audience sits unmoved, waiting to be convinced, involved, and taken with the star. It is her task to stimulate, to break down barriers, to get the message across. There are specific techniques for achievement available to that woman who sets out to make her way in the sales area of marketing. An awareness of those factors, the very dynamics and structure of the typical sales organization and its environment, can be an enlightening experience.

What to Expect

Though no two organizations will approach the management of the personal selling function in the same manner, experience indicates that there are certain common traits that have proved to be typical of many organizations. The woman who seeks to make the most of her personal selling career will be well advised to search for these signposts.

Five Steps of Sales

There are many fine books written on developing the skills of selling; this chapter is not written to encompass anything more than an overview of personal selling, but there are five steps of the selling process you should learn now, as they are the basis of all selling texts.

1. Get the prospect's attention.
2. Arouse interest.
3. Convey the benefits to be achieved by using your product or service.
4. Create desire.
5. Close the sale.

Most functioning sales organizations have a key figure, the sales manager. This person is the planner, the listener, the motivator, the force figure who moves people around the country to gain for the company and for the salesperson the best results in productivity and income. Sometimes the sales manager seems to be the devil at one moment, a protector or overprotector the very next. If you have a strong, fair, personable sales manager as you are starting out on a career in personal selling, it will be a major factor in your success and growth. For that sales manager (most likely a man, although that is changing), the task of integrating women into the sales force can be a tricky one. He may well be used to drinking with the boys, engaging in traditional locker-room activity, seeing women as not suitable to the demands of the road. Obviously what this suggests is that the woman in sales, and that man who most likely will be the one her career success depends on most, will both have to do a lot of rethinking and readjustment if success is to be achieved.

The Great Equalizer

Performance is the great equalizer, the one thing that turns the hard-driving SM into a helpful, open-minded, supportive personality. To the true sales-oriented personality, selling isn't just anything, it is everything. The woman in sales who has that type of person to guide her will find the job a good deal easier.

Skills

Top sales managers analyze the personalities of their people. They seek out those talents that come most naturally, and then blend in those additional skills that experience has indicated are necessary for success. If, for example, a woman feels most comfortable and is successful in face-to-face presentations, but needs help in securing appointments, efforts will be put forth to develop her skills in this door-opening function.

Feedback

No one is his or her own best critic, especially in the sales area. The sales function can be lonely, confusing, and sometimes discouraging, but, thank goodness, often enough rewarding. Just at that moment when the new salesperson has made what appears to be the perfect presentation, following the techniques she has mastered well, and been rejected again, the SM, if he is functioning properly, will close the office door, sit back, and review her activities. The process of feedback, the ability to sit back in an objective manner and assess the performance of a salesperson, is perhaps the most critical and beneficial process in developing your degree of professionalism. In this professional give-and-take, both participants recognize that what is being done is for the purpose of improving performance. Criticism is not given, nor should it be taken, personally.

Sales presents an opportunity for women to earn considerable amounts of money and recognition. This opportunity is not determined by sex, it is determined by skill.

Smart women will be grateful for the opportunity to review what they are doing, to bounce it off someone, as they say in the field, to engage in the interchange of ideas which is the feedback process. All such discussions have a goal. Selling effectiveness is not only rewarding to the individual salesperson, it is also the criterion of performance upon which management and the company are being measured.

Quotas

In order to monitor growth, a company needs to set goals along the way, as well as knowing what is to be achieved at the end of the year. Sales dollar levels, sale quantity of units, orders placed, or other forms of measurement within specified time periods are all valid methods for setting the goals that the organization can be reasonably expected to reach. Sales quotas are usually based on a forecasting method which takes into account such various features as previous performance, the product one is selling, the market climate, the competitive environment, and the length of time the individual salesperson has been working with any one group of accounts and the potential geographic area. Quotas are used to stimulate and measure performance.

Incentives

Closely linked to the quotas that the salesperson will encounter is the incentive system. This is a group or series of rewards of differing types which acknowledge performance and link each achievement above certain minimal standards to specific rewards. The methods companies use to recognize star performers will vary, oftentimes taking the form of cash bonuses, vacations, time off, and even participation in a portion of the company's profits above and beyond certain limits. Stock participation may also be offered as well as certain types of so-called "perks," such as free college or school tuition, a car, and the opportunity to reap the tax benefits that can come with certain types of delayed-compensation arrangements.

Evaluation

In no area of performance within the world of marketing will the tools of evaluation be more continually in evidence than in the sales area. The critical areas in which women in sales can be expected to be judged are threefold: production, growth, and customer relations.

PRODUCTION.   Just how close to or how far in excess of quota will be the woman who has chosen personal selling as her way of life? Though, as the old saw goes, "Liars have been known to figure, but figures don't lie," the point is that unless sales personnel make their figures—and barring any unusual circumstances which might mitigate such performance—the woman who does not measure up to the standards expected of her would be well advised to give her sales career plans an in-depth and forthright reevaluation. Perhaps this career is not for her.

GROWTH.   "Up or out" is the byword of corporate America, and though this is somewhat less the case in the sales department, most companies will be looking to their line sales personnel for their future staff leaders. The ability to get along in the selling environment and to display an ever-broadening knowledge of other areas of the corporation, such as finance, production, future planning, and the like, are sure signs in the evaluation process that the saleswoman will one day be capable of training her successor so that she herself may go on to some greater responsibility.

CUSTOMER RELATIONS.   The successfully operating sales organization will over the years build a reserve of goodwill with its customers that can be of significant assistance to its bottom line. Nothing is as critical to the sales operation as the repeat sale. And for this sale to occur, the personal relationship that will develop in most good professional company-customer encounters that concentrate on the servicing of accounts after the order has been secured is vital. For the woman who truly believes in the importance of personal selling, the key word is *personal*. There is no room for the so-called "after the honeymoon" attitude. Competitors will always be knocking at the door. Taking long-standing accounts for granted can be a costly error.

WHAT KIND OF ORGANIZATION HAVE YOU JOINED?

A peek behind the scenes of several companies' sales organizations suggests that not all sales operations run identically. In the rapidly changing world of business there is constant fragmentation, segmentation, and reorganization of companies, markets, and total industries. Women entering the personal selling area for the first time will have a number of options available to them. There are four major types of selling structures. In many cases, all four, or elements of all four, will be placed in operation. Though no different personal selling skills are required for the execution of each of these, experience suggests that for very subtle reasons, some persons operate better in one of these climates than in any of the others. These reasons will become obvious to the reader as she projects her own evaluation of herself into each of them.

The Territorial Approach

Territorial sales designations encourage the need for the development of personal relations, for one of the primary lessons of marketing is that America is becoming heavily impacted by the customs of regionalism. In the consumer-goods marketplace, the lessons are available daily—what sells in New York may well bomb in Dallas. Mastering the intricacies and peculiarities of a territory, its differences in distribution methods, sales approach, reorder patterns, warehousing systems, and all the thousand-and-one local customs that can, in effect, serve to distinguish it as almost a different country, has been developed to a highly sophisticated level by companies choosing this approach. When feasible, companies will try to place sales talent familiar with an area in that location. The resultant sales organization will usually thus combine the professional elements of a marketing-driven sales operation with the unbeatable extra benefit of home-grown talent.

The Product Approach

Many companies have chosen to assign sales responsibilities according to product type as a method of organization. The reasons are quite simply that it is believed nothing is quite so impressive in a sales call as a well-trained salesperson who knows the ins and outs of her products. In the business climate that exists today, particularly in certain areas of industrial selling and technical sales—computers and the graphic arts are two typical examples—the pleasing personality will not be enough to do the job.

The Specific Market Approach

This type of sales organization seeks to concentrate its efforts against all the possible purchasing requirements of any one industry that it seeks to penetrate. For example, Sales Force A, thoroughly familiar with all the needs of a prospective customer in the financial services area, will be fully prepared to offer insurance, estate planning, and tax counsel, as well as basic accounting services to controllers of small businesses. This form of sales force organization has the benefit of harnessing the basic interests of a salesperson in an area in which she displays a certain degree of expertise, and then extending the line of products offered to maximize the cost efficiency of the sales call when logical interrelationships of one product or service form to another do exist.

The Key Account Approach

This method of sales organization is an outgrowth of and direct response to the centralization of purchasing functions by the customer group responsible for the consumption of certain items. Women who find themselves dealing with organizations in which there are a large number of units doing the same type of thing or offering the same type of activity (discount chains, chain department stores, multistore super-markets) will find that they will be calling on a number of different buyers at company purchasing headquarters. Though each may be re-sponsible for the purchase of a different item, each will be supplying similar customers. Getting to know the different profiles of the key accounts, the manner in which they choose to conduct business, their own marketing goals, cooperative advertising policies, quality stan-dards, and contract specifications can help the new salesperson tre-mendously.

SALES AND THE BROADER
MARKETING PERSPECTIVE

There is no question but that women are demanding, winning, and performing in sales jobs as never before. Notwithstanding this break-through for that woman in sales who views her entry into the ranks of the sales force as but an opening wedge to a career in marketing, the neces-sity to grasp the broader implications of just what she has let herself in for can be helpful. The primary adjustments that will be required of the woman involved in a sales position fall into the area of the attitudes she brings to the job. Spontaneity will very likely be coupled with en-thusiasm and, of course, product knowledge and stick-to-itiveness. She will also be required to discipline herself and to see her function as only a part of the broader scope which is marketing's. In this regard, the ever-present bottom line looms as the most difficult aspect to master. Women, as do their male colleagues, will have to sell with a reason. The modern marketing corporation has defined several criteria for evaluat-ing the efficiency of the selling function. Each is inevitably related at a certain point to profits, though the degree will vary.

Profits:
The End Result

What is the contribution of the sales effort to the bottom line? If it doesn't pay, then the woman in sales will have to find a way to make it pay, by beefing up the closing ratio, increasing sales calls, or concentrating on high-profit items. Whatever the answer, sales—like all of the marketer's other functions—must be held accountable to the demands of profitabil-ity.

What Effect
Does It Have
on Share of Market?

When those who evaluate the performance of the sales force can trace no change in the effectiveness level of certain key marketing mix ingredients—such as product, pricing, sales promotion, and advertising activities—any shift upward in the share of market that the product enjoys may logically and legitimately be attributed to the efforts of the sales operation. Nielsen, in its audit reports on the food and drugstore share of the market, tells the story in the consumer packaged goods area. Any increase in the so-called all-commodity level of store distribution will indicate that the selling efforts of women on the road are successful. In isolating the sales factor from the other variables in the mix, the wise manager will measure the increased levels of the distribution curve and weigh this upward swing heavily in an analysis of profit requirements.

Return
on Assets Management

This last criterion is a method of business control more than it is a yardstick of performance. All those costs related to the sales function—such as salaries, travel and entertainment, promotional literature, direct mail, and the like—are charged against budgeted sales cost figures. With capital being as expensive a commodity as it is in the present climate of high interest rates, the monitoring of expenditures must be a concern to both management and to field sales personnel.

SALES AND THE FUTURE

One of the ongoing discussions I have been privy to when senior managers let down their hair and discuss the future of their own particular organization is, as one might imagine, the ascendency role of different people within different departments of the organization. Putting aside those obvious qualities of leadership, drive, and ambition that are essential if one is to assume a top spot, the case has been well made for other prerequisites. Tight money requires the facility of the financial expert. Technological advance demands those special skills of the manufacturing-bred executive. The control of large numbers of personnel and the management of far-flung corporate empires suggests the talents of the planner. And, of course, the demand end of the marketing equation suggests that the sales personality is best suited to handle the reins of corporate leadership. The woman who dispassionately assesses the ability of a sales career to vault her to the top level of the corporation is no doubt encouraged by the following marketing facts.

Standard of Living

This measure of the public's endless search for the good life keeps escalating at an amazing pace. The land of conspicuous consumption has proven in the last thirty years that with marketing as its driving force, there is no end in sight to the demand for goods and services. The woman who can sell will always have something to sell. Though the forces of the marketplace will be more discriminating and more difficult to read, the adroit saleswoman stands in a position from which she can identify those areas of possible gain; then she can do something to benefit from them. All eyes in the corporation look to her.

Technology as a Cure-all

Though the products and services of the future will no doubt derive in good measure from significant advances in technology, the technocrat is hardly best suited to know just how to apply such progress. His or her distance from the field—the very environment in which constant feedback from consumer and purchaser nurtures the saleswoman—will require reliance on the salesperson to get new advances resulting from technology into distribution.

Human Resources Management

A major area of interest for most management is the proper utilization of personnel. The practical mind of the salesperson is judged to be ideally qualified for the balancing acts required in corporate leadership. With certain exceptions, the marshalling of the skills of hundreds of different types of job experts so as to produce a coherent and realistic product or service, which can then be marketed, is best left to the so-called generalist talents of the sales personality.

In the excellent book *The Managerial Woman*, Margaret Hennig and Anne Jardim suggest that "women, in order to succeed in the corporate world, must be willing to be purposeful in their goals and clear in their desires." Goal achievement and desire fulfillment are nowhere more obtainable than they are via the road marked "personal sales."

5

Marketing in Action: Case Histories

Perhaps one of the most exciting and rewarding aspects of contemporary marketing is that theory has a way of exploding into fact, and the case history that documents the achievements of certain marketers is presented as testimony to a job well done.

Case histories cited in this chapter are only a few from the many available. The criteria for selection are their dynamism and their ability to portray actions that have been accomplished in areas directly related to those major undertakings of the marketing world covered elsewhere in this book.

I chose representative case studies from the consumer goods, retailing, industrial, and service sectors of the marketing world, in order to give you an opportunity to cross-reference and check against data already set down with respect to the philosophy of marketing and how it can be effective in different sectors of the business world.

Each case history will highlight different types of strategies utilized by the marketers chosen. These are experiences of large corporations, which run a wide gamut. Although smaller marketers might have more financial restrictions, their choice of tactics remain wide and varied. Covered are distribution strategy, pricing strategy, product planning and development, and heavy user positioning. Various aspects of several strategy approaches will have contributed to the success of the companies reviewed, though in each case there is a dominant force that has been well thought-through in the planning stages, prior to tactical implementation.

REVLON, INC.:
A NEW POSITIONING,
AND PRICING STRATEGY
LINE EXPANSION

In 1969 this giant of the cosmetics industry embarked upon a strategy for its youth-targeted cosmetics line, Natural Wonder, designed to significantly increase sales volume and to make the product more appealing to a large number of users in the teenage or young adult segment of the marketplace. Prior to this decision to broaden its base, the line, though successful, had a limited positioning because of the short nature and the composition of its product mix. Natural Wonder had been conceived at a time when the cosmetic needs of young women were thought not to go beyond the specialty areas covered by remedial cosmetics such as those used in handling the problems of disturbed skin. Thus the focus of this brand's attention was directed toward acne preparations, spot-cover creams to cover blemishes, and, in general, the entire treatment area of the cosmetics world—one of its three major categories, the others being cosmetics and fragrance.

Research had at that particular time isolated certain signs indicating that with the general loosening in conservative attitudes regarding the wearing of makeup, a previously hidden usage of color products by the younger market segment was beginning to come out in the open. Teenage America was coming of age as part of the revolution of the sixties. With this maturation, the opportunity to position color cosmetics directly to this group, to the expressed interests of this younger segment of the marketplace, became a viable business opportunity. The implications were not lost on the astute Revlon merchants.

Revlon marketing was not so naive as to expect that it had merely to offer new cosmetics products such as lipsticks, nail enamel, eye products, and the like and think that they would be successful. The challenge that faced them was to find some authoritative rationale for broadening Natural Wonder into a complete cosmetics line.

Revlon knew that the change would have to be completed first with those skin-care treatment products that were already a part of the Natural Wonder line. A strategy was evolved which, in retrospect, has all the earmarks of simplicity—and therein lies the seeds of its success. Rather than extolling the merits of Natural Wonder as a line of treatment products that would be kind and gentle to the skin and make it more attractive, the reverse approach was adopted. Revlon reasoned, and properly so, that of the two consumer benefits—beauty and good skin— the former was a more appealing area to pursue. They simply reversed the order of their claim for the products and suggested that Natural Wonder would make the user look more beautiful—and, coincidentally, it would also be good for the skin. After setting this strategic approach, it was then a short and easy step to broaden the base of the products by first introducing a line of lipsticks and, in quick succession thereafter, eye products and nail enamel. The results of this repositioning have made marketing history. Once almost an afterthought line of the company's, conceived originally as a helter-skelter assortment of troubled-skin products, Natural Wonder became a major Revlon brand, among the leaders in the industry catering to the youth segment of the market.

As has been stated, this particular case history places special emphasis on product development as a rationale for the strategy conceived. There are also two subfactors which should be mentioned as having actually contributed significantly to the success of this brand's turnaround. The first has to do with a tactic employed by that company for many of its lines; it was used successfully as a distribution technique throughout the broad range of the company's segmented marketing activities. It is known at Revlon as the process of automatics. Utilizing the sales leverage that the company had achieved by virtue of its success with many different lines of cosmetics, it has been able to ship certain prepackaged and prepriced, standard assortments of merchandise to franchised Revlon accounts on an automatic basis. Merchandise was simply shipped and delivery expected to be accepted, with no prior salesman's call. Introductory deals on new cosmetic items in the Natural Wonder line were designed to get a maximum product exposure with a minimum of costs to the participating retailer and with virtually no Revlon selling cost. It is important to recognize that this technique can only be used in those very special situations when two factors are in operation: The company undertaking such a program must have a strong and very positive relationship with its customers, and customers must be aware that they will be expected to cooperate in certain standard sale areas if they are to share the benefits of larger profits in other areas.

A major factor in the success of this tactic is the ability of a company to design a strategy so exciting that its customers will help to underwrite its initial marketing efforts by offering to cooperate in displaying an item or items that will not return to them their normal profits until some time in the future. The key factor in such strategic planning is an in-depth understanding at the corporate marketing and sales levels of the strength of the company's relationship with its customer network.

The second factor that contributed to the successful broadening of the Natural Wonder line is little spoken about because of the sensitive nature of the topic. It has to do with the less-than-satisfactory performance of some of the earliest lipsticks, which the company introduced under the brand name Natural Wonder Un-Lipsticks. It is a classic from-life example of the way in which an astute marketer can turn a problem into an opportunity and then capitalize on it.

Shortly after the introduction to the trade of the Un-Lipsticks, an unacceptable level of lipstick breakage began to show up in the monitored figures at the Revlon's quality control division. Insisting, as it always had, on unusually high standards of quality control, the company made a decision to recall and replace a staggering number of lipsticks—in sum, 750,000—that were in the field. These had been placed at retail in some 5,000 different outlets. The logistics of such a return were staggering from whatever dimension one wished to view them. Coincidental to this product problem, the company also became aware of some fast-changing color trends in the lipstick marketplace. Fashion executives of the company had been thinking of adding certain new colors to the already existing twenty-seven-shade line so as to take advantage of that fickle thing known as color trends. The decision was made, at some of the highest levels of the company, to immediately recall certain of the lipstick products which did not meet company standards. It was implemented by offering customers a new line of upwards of thirty shades (of course, the new Revlon colors were included). In one broad stroke, an alert marketer had converted a difficult situation into an opportunistic one. The new sell-in and exchange was effected, new shades were introduced, and the economics of the exchange/sales program were profitable.

VLASIC FOODS:
A DISTRIBUTION STRATEGY

Being firm believers that "the proof of the pudding is in the eating" would not have been enough motivation to move this diversified relish-and-condiments company in the direction management had chosen. The marketers at Vlasic Foods set out to add a strategy that could support their line of foods, which featured the rather unglamorous pickle. This strategy would allow them to take major advantage of the superior quality of all of their products.

The strategy focused upon a master plan calculated to emphasize three critical elements in the marketing mix: distribution, regional differences in markets and marketing techniques, and advertising. In each of these areas, the company's utilization of research data— the way, for example, in which they implemented the findings of taste tests and advertising research—enabled the Vlasic marketers to move its pickle line from a 15.9 percent share of the market in 1974 to a dominant number-one-share position of 25 percent against such formidable competitors as Heinz and Del Monte. This successful attempt to take on such giants and best them is unique in its adherence to the fundamentals of marketing. Long a marketer of a full line of relishes and condiments, approximately 150 different products in all, the company sought to break a lead item out of its line for feature showcasing. Building support for this item would have obvious benefits to the rest of the line, which could benefit most from an advertising awareness point of view. The idea was to associate the Vlasic name with a product winner. The policy was chosen as a result of judgments which indicated that the pickle was not the low-interest product which it had been designated. The marketers at Vlasic were convinced the pickles would be responsive to advertising if enough dollars were generated to support a significant advertising effort. They were right. And their product and their packaging were also right. In taste test after taste test, consumers played back their preferences for the Vlasic pickle.

Armed with such data, as well as the regional taste preferences of different parts of the country, the Vlasic marketing professionals chose as their first target four western states: California, Arizona, Utah, and Idaho. While still supporting the brand nationally via network television, the decision was made to implement a regional heavy-up effort in these states, an effort that would include all the elements of the marketing mix. The product was altered to conform to the sweeter pickle taste preferences of the West Coast consumer. Packaging was altered to offer the brand in a consumer-preferred twenty-two-ounce jar rather than the conventional twenty-four-ounce glass container. Sales efforts were stimulated to achieve unusually high distribution levels, approaching 95 percent of all available outlets in these market areas. Advertising levels were heavied up to achieve a greater reach of messages into the prospect consumer group to a point that exceeded the combined advertising reach of all competitors. The results were amazing, as have already been noted. Not only did share increase come about, but the market for pickles was so stimulated that the total market growth was significantly affected.

The lesson for the astute marketer is that concentrated efforts against a small or regional base of operations can pay off. Vlasic, by virtue of concentration, made a market and in the process made itself. The company has since adapted the same principles of concentration, as it has rolled out its regional marketing heavy-up strategy. In each of the market areas it chooses, it has sought to dominate and do an efficient job in that particular market prior to moving on to the next one. The Vlasic story is one of bold thinking linked to a realistic financial plan which has dictated that it is preferable not to undertake the effort unless it can be done properly.

FEDERAL EXPRESS:
A HEAVY-USER STRATEGY

The complexity of doing business in the twentieth century, with the need to manage and get a handle on the data and communications explosion, is the market condition that set the management of Federal Express off on a saga that is the envy of many companies involved in the service sector of our economy. Just several short years ago, senior executives at Federal Express, the nation's largest overnight air parcel service, were quick to recognize that the underservicing of package delivery needs by the available public sector facilities—the post office—and lack of interest and regulatory restrictions on the part of the private sector—the commercial airline industry—left a significant void in the marketplace.

With this judgment gnawing at them, the Federal marketing people set out to determine if the economics of the market potential were significant enough for them to make substantial financial commitments to aircraft, personnel, and advertising. These marketing managers sought, as professionals do, to limit the risks involved by investing, as a first step, in market research efforts that would seek to measure the size of the market, place some dollar value on its potential, and, importantly, to determine if the market could be reached in a sales manner that would be effective and cost-efficient. The answers were positive on all counts. And from this basic research probe emanated the Federal Express success story.

The research effort was centered on isolating that person who was the decision maker—the one who decided from whom parcel delivery services were to be purchased. A probe of the decision-making process revealed that not one but several persons were instrumental in making the decision. Federal marketers judge that even with a small prospective-user base—60,000 accounts in all—the need to reach approximately 250,000 people in order to adequately get their overnight-delivery-service concept across was beyond the reach of their 110-man sales force. The cost per sales call could not possibly pay out. In order to overcome this limitation, the company made the bold decision to use television advertising to reach all of the key decision makers. The cost effectiveness of television, even though it is by nature less persuasive and more wasteful than is the personal selling method, was still sufficient to tilt the marketing judgment in its favor. At this stage in the market development of the company, testing had verified that a prospective purchaser could be motivated by television. What remained was to narrow the gap and make television sales-call dollars as effective and productive as possible. So the Federal people went back to research.

By utilizing the Standard Industry Classification Code (SIC), which categorizes all American business enterprise by type of business conducted, Federal marketers were able to probe the overnight parcel usage rate of various broad industrial sectors. For example, they were able to determine that a company engaged in the printing industry had ten times greater usage levels of overnight air parcel service than did a soft drink bottler. With this data in hand, clever market research analysis sought to isolate those prospective users by their geographic location. This was accomplished by a cross-referencing of employment figures by industry as against city of employment. The result was an index of buying-power potential which afforded Federal an accurate profile of who their most likely buyer was and where he or she was located. The pattern that emerged was that of a traditional, heavy-user group. Forty percent of users accounted for upwards of 60 percent of usage. The heavy users were concentrated in just twenty-three cities, thus making the planning of advertising efforts a much more scientific undertaking.

Federal has expanded its business significantly since its original market entrance. Its current advertising expenditures are at the multimillion-dollar level, and sales promotion efforts in support of its ongoing selling effort against new users are budgeted in excess of a million dollars annually. The problems of marketing to a limited-user group are overcome by the utilization of direct mail and other promotional techniques. They have proved to be the most cost-efficient also.

Federal Express is a prime example of a research-originated, heavy-user marketing strategy. The research role cannot be undervalued—indeed, management credits it with much of the company's success. The route restrictions of commercial airlines, their daytime passenger-schedule bias, and their lack of facilities to pick up and deliver on either end of the airplane trip continue to keep them at a safe and noncompetitive distance. Though the post office has made some competitive inroads, smart marketers everywhere concede that the long-term edge goes to Federal. It has been an overnight success in an overnight business.

MACY'S NEW YORK PRODUCT PLANNING AND DEVELOPMENT

Accurate and on-target strategic planning for retailers is one of the most difficult of marketing tasks. Tough enough in a marketplace that is forever coming up with new forms of merchandise distribution— witness the generic discount store, Sunday openings, convenience stores, and the like—it is believed by most experts to be a doubly difficult task when the challenge is to turn around a faltering operation of a once-leading retail operation. The marketers at R. H. Macy's flagship Herald Square store in New York City—reputed to be the world's single largest shopping area, and at one time in a position of dominance in the nation's largest city—were having their troubles.

Buffeted by low-price competitors who drained off the middle-class shopper's dollar with huge values in the women's and children's ready-to-wear areas, and faced with a general deterioration of its customer base because of a variety of socioeconomic factors, the store appeared to be heading toward disaster. An intensive executive study of the long-term trends in the area convinced the retailer's marketing management that its location, though itself deteriorating, did offer opportunities for turnaround because of the store's fortunate access to mass transportation. In a city that depends on mass transit, the subway and the bus, to move its millions back and forth daily, Macy's management reasoned that it was the store's task to find new ways to attract customers, regardless of their physical location. With the right mix of merchandise working hand in hand with the right mix of transportation facilities, the customer would come. The scope of this undertaking is best exemplified by some of the statistics that attest to customer traffic. Actual counts by store personnel reveal that on a busy day, it is not unheard of for upward of a quarter of a million persons to pass through the store's various departments.

The Macy approach focused on two marketing aspects: a redesign of the interior of the store to make it an easier and more pleasurable place to shop, and a realignment of certain merchandise areas, paying close attention to the specific merchandise needs of its core middle-class customers.

If the merchandise development plan can be said to have been successful, no small part of the success has been attributed to the planning process involved in changing the retailing environment itself. Opting to throw its somewhat staid, if reliable, image aside, Macy's sought to lure the younger, trend-setting customer and—in a bold commitment of funds, approximately $10 million—sought to embrace the "retailing as theater" concept, which seeks to lure the shopper to the excitement of the shopping environment it created. It worked. Starting with a magnificent renewal of its bargain basement area, subsequently named "The Cellar," it created a shopping spectacular full of individual shops, restaurants, and other entertainments which literally riveted the customer's attention by clever use of display, signage, and merchandise in use settings. More an interior designer's fantasy than a traditional retailer's layout for efficient space utilization, the results were far in excess of even that venerable store's most optimistic management. At first year's end, sales for the Herald Square unit were up 10 percent, and an entire generation of young, new-user shoppers had cemented a relationship with the store which could reasonably be expected to last a good many years.

SAVIN BUSINESS MACHINES: A MULTIFACETED STRATEGY

The Valhalla, New York, based copying machine company has rested its case in the copying field on its choice of marketing as the leading edge of its business effort, as contrasted to the technological and manufacturing bias that is the province of the leader, Xerox. In the process a company with a pretax loss of $5 million as recently as 1976 has turned this performance around to generate profits in the area of $20 million to $25 million. Though not the volume equals of giant Xerox, the Savin group achieved the distinction of exceeding the competition's unit placement rate, and thus found itself in 1977 with in excess of one third of the units placed by the combined sales efforts of all the leaders, including Xerox and IBM. This is no meager achievement given the circumstances of the market, but less unlikely than might be thought if one reviews the marketing thinking that motivated the efforts. Up against a major, well-entrenched competitor, the Savin group sought to do almost everything in the copying business in a manner directly opposite to what had become the Holy Grail for the industry. They did it magnificently. The key factor in their success was a careful analysis of the needs of the marketplace for copying machines. The market had been characterized by rapid change as the proliferation of need for copying within the business community continued to escalate. The pyramid effect of the need to copy changed the nature of the market from that of a quality reproduction bias to one that emphasized the need for geographic convenience to the copying machine. Savin was ready with a low-priced competitor that effectively enabled an owner to buy two copying machines for the price he had been paying for one.

The production in terms of copying fidelity of the Savin liquid toner unit versus the powder-generated reproduction of the Xerox competitor, though not as truthful, was not a stumbling block. Savin's accurate market readings enabled them to sell the virtues of multiple-machine placement. The less sophisticated Savin unit was also easier to service; the net result was a very salable package which had at its core a cheaper, near-parity product with a more reliable record for service. The Savin marketing orientation also paid significant dividends in the manner in which the Savin machine was sold. Eschewing the cost-intensive proprietary sales force method, Savin chose instead to strengthen and build its existing dealer network. In the process it was able to place upwards of 1,900 sales representatives on the road, supported by a generous, all-commission remuneration package and a sale versus rental financial arrangement that was more in keeping with the independent dealers' cash-flow capabilities. The last, but equally important, plank in the Savin marketing strategy was to generate awareness for the Savin name among prospective purchasers. These efforts to secure leads and soften the territory for salesmen making cold calls were achieved by linking the Savin name somewhat irreverently with the leader, Xerox, in much of the Savin advertising. The head-to-head confrontation almost overnight placed a little-known name in the same league as the giant. And the soundness of the competitive selling story Savin presented had the effect of making the buyer ponder a second choice.

Savin is currently cementing its dealer-organization relations, as it is apparent to company management that the future growth of the corporation will depend as much on this network of operators as on any of the technological advances the company's R & D efforts can hope to produce. An active dealer cooperative-advertising program provides for company-shared expenditures for both media-related and direct mail efforts.

Savin has proven the point. Given some sort of an opening in the structure of a product category and its pricing, a clever and aggressive marketing posture backed by a total commitment on the part of marketing professionals can indeed make inroads in product areas where before others had feared to tread.

Multistrategy approaches perhaps best describe these case histories. They are a confirmation of the fact that the right solution to a marketing problem involves an integration of a number of proven techniques and tools. I've always believed that it is the *cumulative* impact that leads to success, rather than any single action.

II

NEW DIRECTIONS
IN MARKETING

6

Marketing for the Nonprofit Organization

For those individuals who face what seems an uphill fight to gain the experience employers are always asking for, but rarely seem willing to offer, this chapter should be of particular interest. The nonprofit organization offers a unique training ground to hone one's marketing skills on a part-time or full-time basis. The goals of these groups are not measured in the normal dollars-and-cents yardsticks of business, but in the medical, legal, social, cultural, and educational benefits that can be gained by the public. The decade of the 1980s is bringing into focus the need of these organizations, from local to national, to market their message in the most professional manner possible, utilizing the latest techniques and tools.

Employment in a nonprofit organization can be on two levels, volunteer or salaried. Both will bring fulfillment, but the latter can be a high-intensive education. It is intensive because the usual nonprofit marketing situation is one of minimal staff, small budgets, high pressure, and many hats to be worn by few people, if not only one.

The nonprofit sector has started to utilize certain aspects of the marketing concept in order to be more efficient, effective, and result-oriented in what is constantly being referred to as turbulent times. Some of the factors causing this shift from past practices are outlined below.

Attitude Shift

The emergence of the middle class as an ever-increasing and powerful consumer group, the broad populist movement in the country, and the effects and persuasive reach of communications—television in particular—have broadened the market demand for so-called social goods and services to the point where large numbers of persons are involved. University attendance, museum art appreciation, medical research, civic involvement, political action, social programs, and symphony orchestra attendance are no longer limited, elitist-only options. The demand for these activities has grown tremendously.

Tax Structure

In varied ways, the tax system allows for deductions to nonprofit organizations. Benefactors are concerned that these bequests are managed in an efficient manner, a manner consistent with the very same successful business activities that allowed for their accumulation in the first place.

In addition, there are from time to time dire predictions that the tax structure might be readjusted to the detriment of nonprofit groups. Thus another reason for increased marketing skills—for the acts of getting more out of the public and influencing government to do less are damaging the foundations on which nonprofit efforts are built.

Exposure

The clear-cut lines that for years served as a barrier between the commercial and noncommercial worlds have faded. Today there is a cross-pollenization of activities between these two sectors, which inevitably leads to an opening of eyes. Each of the sectors has seen the wisdom in borrowing from the other. For example, the rapidly growing, sophisticated techniques and tools of direct marketing have been adopted and adapted by a wide range of groups, from ballet to those concerned with medical research.

Sales promotion and public relation activities have been integrated into the efforts of universities to raise funds, recruit students, and place graduates with companies throughout the world. Fine art is finding its way into everything from fashions to high-profit mail order offers. Original works of art may show up, courtesy of a museum, in a retail store promotion, as might a company throw a bash for a new-product introduction at a cultural institution. The skills of the display decorator are influencing curators so they can attract the maximum number of museum visitors.

Accountability

The realities of a hard-pressed, inflation-impacted market make the burden of accountability a more formidable one for today's nonprofit organization administrator. These are indeed difficult times. There is a constant reevaluation of priorities taking place in the allocation of funds. It is not unheard of to close previously sacrosanct institutions. Library hours are shortened to provide additional dollars for adequate police protection. Gentlemen of the pulpit are forced to fill that church every Sunday; their tenure is questioned if they cannot do so. Charitable organizations, those that benefit sick persons, orphans, the drug-culture impacted, are forced to strict accountability by overseers and boards of directors whose business experience has taught them what things should cost.

The net result of these influences has led logically to the marketer. She or he has demonstrated that in the world of profit there are indeed better and more professional ways to do things. The nonprofit sector has matured to the point at which it seeks to maximize its social profits by maximizing its marketing skills. Being on a nonprofit basis should no longer be sufficient reason to explain dwindling symphony attendance or decreased public contributions.

Degrees
of Nonprofit Marketing

The question of which marketing techniques to adopt with respect to different types of nonprofit activities is an interesting and complex one. Far from eliminating any of the basic marketing functions—price, distribution, product/service, advertising, sales promotion, public relations, market research—the task of the nonprofit marketer is to know which of this group or which combinations are best suited to their marketing undertaking. The choice of marketing techniques is therefore a much more difficult one, involving the reactions of many different publics than those encountered by the profit-sector marketer.

THE NEED
FOR FULL-SCALE MARKETING

Hospitals for years have been tremendously neglectful of those things a for-profit business would never ignore, that is, customer service, image, productivity, and finances. Fortunately for many citizens, hospitals have now found themselves in a competitive situation in that in addition to those that are run on a nonprofit basis, private industry has entered the market, providing modern management techniques and skills combined with the finest quality medical service, and has turned hospitals into a for-profit situation.

As is true in any free market system, competition is healthy for the public as a whole. Now hospitals have been forced to attract better-skilled administrators, and the quality of health care in the nonprofit area has increased substantially. Many hospitals that for years ran into the red now are faced with competition from the private sector, and are doing everything possible to show a reserve at the end of the year without being detrimental to their service. For profit or not, any substantial organization such as a hospital should be putting forth a maximum marketing effort to operate on an efficient, professional level. Persons who are expected to pay a fee for the treatment (service/product) should feel that they are getting the best possible deal. The reasons for this are obvious. The cost of health-care delivery in many parts of this country has escalated to the point where it is beyond the reach of many average citizens. Fees go up because costs go up. The cost of nonprofessional and professional workers, food, medical care, medication, medical specialization, and the sophisticated equipment necessary calls loudly for the adoption of sound business practices. Marketing techniques encompassing advertising to public relations to motivation and more, in relationship to management practices, patient relations, fund raising, and cost-effective operations, play a role in the total management policy of a hospital that will operate at full efficiency, maximum productivity, and with a consistent performance relating to its community image.

Another solid example of a concentrated marketing approach would be that of the Muscular Dystrophy Association. Their goal is to eradicate the disease. The vehicle is money—for research, rehabilitation, and treatment. There will be few readers who are not familiar with the efforts put forth by the MDA with Jerry Lewis involving the techniques of advertising, public relations, and, in particular, sales promotion, for generating awareness, funds, and volunteers, while at the same time building morale and stimulating those who are struggling to find a cure for this horrible disease.

GETTING BY—MARKETING ON A SMALLER SCALE

Where hospitals and the Muscular Dystrophy Association require use of maximum marketing techniques, there are those situations that utilize a more moderate level of intensity in their efforts. These are the nonprofit organizations that operate on a smaller scale, on a local or regional basis, such as a library, museum, zoological association, or committee or foundation concentrating on an area of interest and of social concern to a particular region. Quite often these organizations offer the public something at little cost. They require the support of outside donations as well as federal grants in order to add an element of enjoyment or "civilization" to their particular geographic area. Some of the marketing techniques utilized by these groups are public relations in the form of press releases, public speaking engagements, and events taking place at their location or on behalf of their organization. They use advertising on a limited basis, plus a good portion of those items in the marketing mix, such as product/service—that is, paintings, animals at the zoo, slide shows, concerts, repertory theater, and much more. There is also the distribution aspect of the mix as to where the goods will be inventoried, how they will be shipped, and who will distribute them to the general public. And of course, as we mentioned earlier, they must consider the communications aspect with advertising and promotion.

A level of marketing intensity that is a softer effort can be related to volunteer organizations such as a local church, a local symphony orchestra, or perhaps a fund-raising event for a goal that, once achieved, will not repeat itself. Here the various interactions of the group, with its many publics, have to be taken into consideration, even though the work relating to a volunteer organization may seem small-scale compared to that of a major corporation. The pressures and needs for marketing skills are in proportion to many of the country's largest marketing firms. The pastor of a church has to be a spiritual leader while at the same time being an adroit politician in order to interrelate with the many community boards of officialdom that have a direct effect on parishioners. The leader of a fund-raising group has to have the skills of persuasion and personal selling to get the local newspaper or radio or television stations to give coverage to their efforts. In order to insure that literature is distributed to the right groups at the right time can be more difficult than one might imagine. So the volunteer marketers will have their job cut out for them, even at this level.

A similar situation exists with private schools and colleges, museums, and charity organizations, which rely heavily on the use of marketing techniques in the raising of funds to achieve their goals and objectives. The gathering of funds is usually the responsibility of the individual concerned with most marketing activities. These efforts will range from obtaining government grants to direct-mail appeals to charity balls, and more. All will have one thing in common: The marketing plan, the tools and techniques utilized, will be for the short term. Specific projects within certain time periods, with predetermined goals (in dollar amounts), communication skills—writing, public relations, persuasion, selling . . . even advertising—all are factors that the nonprofit marketer will use in this facet unique to the nonprofit sector.

It is valuable to understand what marketing is and what it can do at all levels of personal or community activities. PTA, local theatre groups, small art museums, local fire departments—all have marketing needs. Politicians and the governments they run, large and small, require marketing activities. Most will fall into the "occasional" situation, perhaps once or twice a year. But when they do, the degree of importance is equal to that of any large corporation. Again, the basic tools of persuasion and communication come into play.

Effective Tools for the Nonprofit Marketer

Though the nature of the nonprofit organization has its subtle and substantive differences from those that affect the profit sector, certain basic techniques can be used by both.

STRATEGIC PLANNING.   The concept of long-term growth, supported by a tactical structure that can be utilized at various stages during growth development, is ideally suited for the nonprofit organization. The college president who has no vision of the educational needs of a changing student body cannot hope to mount an effective fund-raising drive for the university. The museum director who wishes to build attendance, raise funds, and sustain membership growth has to think long-range in order to achieve these goals. Planning, forecasting, innovating, and promoting are skills necessary for the success of a nonprofit organization. A fact of life is that the competition for the public's attention and dollars is intensifying from all sectors; those who plan better than others will survive—and grow.

PUBLIC RELATIONS.   The need to affect public perceptions and opinion is of vital importance to the nonprofit sector. The publicity activities of the famed King Tut exhibit, with significant television, newspaper, and magazine coverage, provided an excellent example of how imaginative public relations efforts can be utilized to increase museum attendance. The tie-ins of the Muscular Dystrophy Association with corporate-sponsored events magnifies their message at little cost. Its form can vary from situation to situation, ranging from simple, well-planned press releases to the super event, for example, a formal charity ball. Public relations is credibility—a substantial factor in building.

SALES PROMOTION.   A marketing technique more often thought of in conjunction with fast-food operations and package-goods firms, sales promotion can be a powerful weapon in the arsenal of the nonprofit organization. These tactics include couponing to draw attendance, premiums to sell memberships, and posters for fund raising. Sales promotion is often called the measurable medium, for its main purpose is to motivate someone to take action—and that is the name of the game in a nonprofit sector.

DISTRIBUTION. An effective distribution system is a very effective tool for nonprofit organizations. Distribution can refer to any format of the printed word when the concern is dissemination of information, such as at conventions, caucuses, and rallies—for example, distribution of literature that highlights the purpose and activities of a nonprofit group, or distribution of materials to be utilized for fund raising—that is envelopes, instructions, products to be sold. Distribution relates to any effort that enables a segment of the marketing activity to be delivered somewhere—posters on bulletin boards, bibles in hotel rooms, banners in strategic places. All form another necessary link in the marketing chain.

Guarding the Future
of Nonprofit Marketing

There is much that remains unanswered within the broad area of nonprofit marketing, as it is a rapidly changing marketplace. The method of training available to that woman who would choose this arena of marketing work would best seem to be the fundamentals of basic profit-oriented marketing. The transfer of such skills to the nonprofit sector should be done with caution and careful consideration. The delicate balance that separates the two sectors must always be kept in mind, for the short-term expediencies of the profit sector do not always work in nonprofit. It does take a different kind of calling if the proper servicing of the public need is to be satisfied. Personal opinion, and that only, suggests that such persons will be commercial enough to seize the utility offered by the marketers' skills, and yet selfless enough to forego some of the more obvious areas of commercialism. Without this latter attribute the balance the nonprofit organization intends—indeed, is chartered to provide within the American mix of products and services—may well suffer the fate of overcommercialization.

7

Marketing for the Professional Service Organization

The professional service organization encompasses businesses based on supplying advice, information, and aid in the fields of medicine, law, engineering, accounting, investments, management science, research, and other areas considered academic or intellectual in tone. Among these are included the physician, the attorney, the dentist, the accountant, the marketing consultant, the broker, the management consultant, the pure researcher, the architect. No single event in the last twenty years has been more reassuring to those companies and individuals who have embraced and been successful with the incorporation of the marketing approach into their business activities than its apparent maturation into a field long thought of as too esoteric, too unspecific, too immeasurable, too unstable, and too unquantifiable.

Professional services are subject to the planning and management that marketing offers, but certain accommodations must be made in those techniques used to approach it. This chapter will use the marketing consultant as a specific example of how the task of marketing such professional services can best be accomplished.

There are certain very specific reasons underlying the emergence of the professional service group as a candidate for marketing's skills. These have to do essentially with a basic shift in the economics of the times. In developed countries, a shift toward consumer gratification in the service sector—as represented by the buyer's desire for better health care, adequate legal protection, and a more meaningful utilization of financial resources—has altered the way in which economic entities spend their dollars.

THE TIME IS NOW

An important reason for the explosion in demand for professional services has been the trend toward industrial diversification which today's business community adheres to. More different types of business, housed under the umbrella of one controlling financial center or source, require that the organization that has embarked on such a horizontal spread of its activity reach out beyond the scope of its own personnel for the skills of the professional. Specialists are needed in marketing, accounting, and pure research, to name but a few areas.

As astute marketers already know, the identification of a consumer or buyer need is but the first step in the marketing process that seeks to satisfy it. In the area of professional services the task has been complicated by the attitude of society, which for many years has sought to define the professional's right for adequate remuneration as a negligible factor.

The realities of the need to sell to survive broke the barriers that had hindered such professional services purveyors. Thus, effective efforts were mounted to apply many of the marketing techniques which had served so well in the consumer and industrial sectors to the marketing problems of the professional service person or organization.

IDENTIFYING
THE PROFESSIONAL

To identify the professional, six characteristics are used, as originally outlined by Frances Bennion in his book, *Professional Ethics*. Together with the definition of a service, which the American Marketing Association defines as "credentials, benefits or satisfactions which are offered for sale," they tend to further delineate the special marketing approach that must be taken to the marketing of professional services. These characteristics are:

> *Intellectual bias:* A tested-by-trial-and-error theory that lends itself to specific discipline and requires formal education in its specialities.
>
> *Private practice:* A derivation of the professional's skills in one-to-one client relationships, with remuneration in the form of fees from individuals rather than a salary.
>
> *Advisory function:* Acting as counsel, often coupled with some executive responsibilities in actual execution phases, both with full responsibility for results vested in the professional advisor.
>
> *Tradition of service:* An objective, public-good attitude which subordinates the making of money as secondary.

Representative institute: A society of member professionals who safeguard, accredit, and maintain certain agreed-upon standards of competency.

Code of conduct: The hows, wherefores, whys, and why nots as they regard the conduct of the professional member of the representative institute.

PLACING A MARKET VALUE ON THE PROFESSIONAL

Inasmuch as the pricing mechanism that operates for goods manufactured in the consumer or industrial sectors is influenced in most instances by demand, the ingredients that affect the establishment of such prices are affected by a large body of data. Much of the pricing of such components has a very specific relationship to the durability and commitment of the product. With this as a standard, the marketer of professional services is forced to compare the value of his or her services against it. The situation is obviously a difficult one, for the comparison would appear to be as between apples and oranges. Intensive research has indicated that this is not the case, and it is upon a relative measurement of the following three areas of consumer/industrial goods value that the pricing of professional services is based.

Durability

Although one might at first find it difficult to comprehend this concept in the purchase of a professional service, logic will show it to be true. The duration of the marketing consultant on a project may be short-term, but if he has done his work well, the result will be long-term—durable. The purchaser of a professional service is making a durable investment that will accrue dividends to him just as does the making of a durable investment in equipment. Where a purchase is made for equipment to produce plastic bottles faster and more cost-efficient you have an easier-to-understand example of durability. Keep in mind that the shape, size, label, and packaging of that bottle may have been decided on from the input and expertise of the marketing consultant. The marketing consultant whose skills allow him to prescribe the proper positioning of a product against its competition is performing a durable service that will reward the marketer in the form of a profitable product whose financial gain he can take advantage of. The selling strategy that caused the demand for the product in the bottle, and thus the need for new equipment, might have been heavily influenced by the marketing consultant's recommendations. Though the purchase of the professional service was for a limited time, the effect shows a longer and stronger durability and a value for which proper compensation can be made.

Tangibility

You can also measure the value of the professional's service on its tangibility merit. Look at the aspect of utility in the services performed. The marketing consultant's skills do have a degree of utility, and thus tangibility: he makes recommendations that isolate potential customer benefits or identify competitors (or their own) weaknesses, he suggests direction that provides management with defined parameters in the decision-making process. These are major tangibles that allow the purchaser to feel he has received value for his expenditures for the skills of the professional service firm.

Commitment

When management decides to purchase X tons of raw material, or lease Y number of trucks, they are making a clear example of a commitment. When they consider the financial commitment to a professional service firm, it is more difficult for them to understand, especially if the service is not essential. Can it still be worth paying for? Certainly! Consider market research. A consultant can search out the magnitude of one market segment against another. The marketer can live without the cost if nothing of value shows. But, if research indicates there is a greater demand for the product among certain target groups than others, the marketer will have received strong value because his direction can be more rifle-targeted than shotgun in approach. The old axiom about insurance relates here to a commitment to the professional service firm: "It's better to have it and not need it than to need it and not have it."

With this rationale for a value placement on the marketing of professional services in place, it is prudent to examine the ways in which the marketer of professional services will have to alter basic marketing techniques in order to confront the realities of the intangibles to be offered. In this regard a singular debt is owed to Warren J. Wittench, who outlined what are essentially three keystone areas of a marketing rationale for professional services in an article in the *Harvard Business Review*, "How to Buy/Sell Professional Services."

SPECIAL CONCEPTS
AFFECTING PROFESSIONAL
SERVICES MARKETING

There is an aura of differentiation that affects the marketer who wishes to market professional services. These differentiations are somewhat nonspecific in definition; though, in the broadest sense, those marketing strategies which will be implemented to market the service itself will derive essentially from the concept of marketing as applied in the consumer goods sector, the special characteristics mean that the professional services marketer will have to take into account certain special considerations in approaching his or her task.

> *Minimizing uncertainty:* Professional services must add a strong degree of confidence to the business undertakings of its clients.
>
> *Understanding problems:* Professional services must understand the totality of the fundamentals of the client's business.
>
> *Buying the professional:* The sale of ability, charm, and personal persuasiveness is icing on the cake, but by itself is meaningless in the decision of a prospective purchaser to opt for the services of a professional. It is skill and accomplishment that count.

Given this brief overview of development of the professional services movement, its definition, distinguishing characteristics, and a perspective as to its orientation, it is important to move on to more specific territory. Utilizing actual data gathered from the confidential files of a leading marketing counseling firm, a case history development will outline the marketing efforts of this organization which have been successful.

MARKETING CONSULTANT
CASE HISTORY

IDENTIFICATION OF PROSPECT NEED.   Counselor X apparently gave considerable thought to her marketing technique. Analysis indicates that prior planning played a considerable role in her process. Her organization directed its initial marketing efforts to research activities that sought to isolate those prospective companies most likely to employ its services. The results of this research indicated a very specific target group. Prime characteristics of this group were a bias toward production, limited sales force capability, innovative new-product development, low consumer/customer awareness, minimal interdepartmental coordination, somewhat remote geographic location, and the absence of a formal program of industry information gathering. Seeing these voids in the operations of a considerable number of business organizations led the consultant service to develop the elements of a positioning philosophy for the marketing of its own professional services.

NAMING THE SERVICE.   The consultants chose to position their group as one that would provide its service as an additional benefit to prospective customers. The name *Supplemental* was chosen as being the one that could most rapidly communicate the nature of those services which were being offered. Under this umbrella, the consultant chose to further clarify the tangibility aspect and the durability and commitment components of its services by outlining a specific list of services available as a part of its program. Namely, these were intelligence gathering, analysis, and evaluation; the identification of goals; the identification of new markets for existing products; methods of increasing business from current customers; new-product development; and, of course, strategic planning.

SPELLING OUT WHAT THE SERVICE IS NOT.   In an area that leans so heavily for acceptance on bringing confidence to the operations of the prospect company, the consultant sought to minimize any reservations the prospect might have as to the nature of the activities and scope of the consulting organization and its specific difference as contrasted to overlapping, same-sounding types of professional service organizations. The consultants' presentation approach scrupulously outlined its noninvolvement, albeit noninterest in the personal assessment, and restructuring functions which are often the core activities of the management consultant group. The consultant focused its presentation efforts on the catalytic nature of its presence. The ability of the supplemental group to maximize the contributions of company staff personnel by providing a counseling attitude and atmosphere was the chief attitudinal aspect of the approach to business that was communicated. Such efforts were rewarding. Without them the confidence levels of prospective buying groups would have been seriously tested.

Benefits Derived
from Employing the Consultant

The manner and form of actual implementation of the services of the consultant group were judged to be an important area to explain to prospective customers. If these prospects were to feel comfortable about integrating the consultant into their operations, they would have to be convinced that such a relationship could indeed be set up in such a manner that the consultant would be privy, without benefit of staff discomfort, to all those areas of the prospect customer's business which it had a need to know. Several factors were emphasized, the most important of them being the entire area of confidentiality. The consultant was convinced that a fiduciary relationship with its clients, much like the confidential relationship that exists between a doctor and his patient or an attorney and his client, must exist if the consultant was to be in a clear position to have his counsel heeded. The consultant therefore set up an exclusive, nonconflicting arrangement which functioned as a primary factor in all of its relations. It would only develop or foster relationships with one client in any single category of business. Starting with this attitude as a given, the consultant further sought to demonstrate, via presentation, the scope of its marketing skills. This was accomplished by reducing to broad conceptual areas those marketing techniques that could effectively be applied regardless of company type. Additionally, the consultant's marketing efforts sought to communicate the value of the concept of supplemental thinking, as follows:

OPENING THE CLOSED ENVIRONMENT.   The third-party discipline of loyal opposition thought was offered as a noncompeting tool to stimulate creative thinking. In this area the consultant stressed the singular ability to extend the client's horizons by introducing concepts learned in other client relationships which might have application to any one particular client's business. The focus of the consultant's marketing efforts was to demonstrate the authenticity of innovative development as a direct result of so-called open-skies thinking.

ASSET DEPLOYMENT.   The consultant was further successful in a presentation of its case for the maximization of human resources based on the factors of availability and cost. Given the nature of the consultant's prospect customer groups' size and the average prospect company's staff composition, the consultant emphasized the à la carte nature of the service offerings. Specifically, programs were structured in such a way that a client could utilize all or part of the marketing services available through the consultant group. Great care was taken to insure management that no disruption of employed, on-board staff would be recommended. The concept conveyed was that existing personnel could be most productive by continuing to function at those tasks they were most familiar with. Certain minimal dollar commitments were set as a requirement of the arrangement. Without them the consultant judged the sincerity of its relationships to be in question. What was to be emphasized was the flexibility built into the consultant's offerings.

Checklist for
Consultant Retention

The consultant's marketing efforts paid considerable attention to knowing when a prospective client was in a position to benefit from the retention of outside counsel. Research on executive habits at the senior management level isolated the timing factor, that is, the ability to set aside time to think and to plan as being the most critical problem facing top management. Studies indicated that an awareness of the pressing need to cope with the immediate, short-term problems of business operations impacted heavily on the thinking time of these executives. The acknowledgment that only the absence of time available to be devoted to planning might stand in the way of growth and success was repeated in interview after interview. The consultant utilized this finding to stress those tradeoffs made in the name of dollar expediency. Here the consultant was frank to affirm that no guarantees of return on investment in a consultant time commitment would be forthcoming. Nonetheless, the specter of the possibility of losing the opportunity to benefit was a compelling enough factor to make the consultant's argument a significant one.

CREDIBILITY.   Perhaps the most persuasive sales argument for consultant retention can be found in the area of credibility. A review of available data suggests that in the case of this marketing consultant, a presentation approach which stressed the need of the client to be confronted with opinions that might be contrary to accepted wisdom was of paramount value. The consultant in this case shrewdly assessed the other- or dissenting-voice capability. It was this independent attitude that convinced many clients an investment in outside counsel could add an extra and needed dimension to company operations.

Three final areas of inspection are necessary for a clear understanding of all the factors involved in the marketing of consultant services. Before going into them, it should be noted that making known the availability of consultant or professional services is subject to the same techniques of communication that the consumer-goods sector utilizes to sell its products. With certain modifications to allow for industry practice and accepted law and standards of conduct, the marketing consultant, lawyer, dentist, and others in the professional service category are today utilizing advertising, promotion, and public relations techniques of a variety of forms to cement the lines of sales communications between their service and their prospective clients. In bringing the skill of the marketer to such market development, the service organization or professional services individual would do well to retain outside counsel who will be aware of the latest institutional thinking as it effects marketing for any one specific group.

Cementing
the Professional Service
Client Agreement

With the basics at least conceptually outlined for placing a value on professional services, the closing of the sale is every much a bit of the overall marketing strategy effort of the service group as is the positioning of its logical fit vis à vis its prospect. Fee structuring, the realities of the overhead problem, and the specifics of the client relationship are important.

FEE STRUCTURING.   Any number of arrangements are available to the service organization. Retainer fees are preferred by some because of the commitment required by the participating parties. Combination retainers and override fees for specific projects are also included as part of the fee-arrival procedure. And, of course, there is a flat fee per project undertaken which is preferred by many clients whose cost accounting methods are applied to all company undertakings. Fee-structuring activities must be attentive to the different capabilities of different clients. Other factors must be taken into account, including such things as the repeat capability of the client, the desirability of working within certain types of industry that may open opportunities in related industries, and the exposure to some highly visible clients which would afford new areas of knowledge to the service group not otherwise attainable.

REALITIES OF OVERHEAD.   Arriving at a formula for fee assignment, the service organization must deal with the realities of overhead—rent, light, telephone, travel, entertainment, and the like. To this basic group of indirect costs, the time, as accounted for by direct wage per salary payments of service group employees, must be added. A rule of thumb that has stood the test of time for many service groups is to triple the direct cost of labor assigned to the servicing of an account. The resultant figure will, given a level of normal overhead expenditures, result in a profit before taxes of approximately 6 percent.

THE CONTRACT.   Supplier-client contracts are vital to the healthy functioning of service groups' client relationships. With few specifics to cost on the budget sheets, it is important to know exactly what is to be expected of each party in the relationship. Broad areas that should be covered in such contracts are as follows:

> *Description of project:* Whatever is to be undertaken should be clearly defined.
>
> *Participating personnel:* In many cases, the service groups' retention will rest on the availability of certain key personnel. Those persons who will participate in the actual work involved in the project and the nature of their duties should be specified.
>
> *Client responsibilities:* Service organizations will be wise to specify the area and the persons within those areas who will serve as a contact point for interface within the client organization.
>
> *Time frame:* Timetabling of activities from start through completion date must be specified.
>
> *Disputes:* With respect to the fulfillment of obligations on the part of each of the parties, an avenue of mediation should be included which calls upon the judgment of a third party. Normal arbitration procedures can be delegated to those established forums available in industry associations.
>
> *Payments:* The scheduling of payments should be spelled out as to specific dates.

As I indicated at the beginning of this chapter, I approach the marketing of a professional service as it could be used within a marketing consultancy, obviously, because of my familiarity with this particular industry. It takes only a quick review of the basic characteristics outlined—for example, durability, tangibility, commitment, etc.—to convert similar situations to your particular industry or service. Remember, whether your primary income is derived from selling graphic arts, copy, legal services, or from any of the occupations that fall into the service category, the marketing philosophy as outlined in this chapter, when properly applied, can be easily adapted to your particular situation.

EMBARKING ON A CAREER IN MARKETING

8
Strategy for Embarking on A Career in Marketing

A not-so-quiet revolution is taking place. Women, in increasing numbers, have entered the executive suites of America's and the world's corporations as never before. From each sector of society, with a broad variety of personal goals and aspirations, the day of the woman as marketer, entrepreneur, second-income earner, leader, aggressive and assertive personality, is here.

Why it has happened, how it has happened, and what chance a woman with this determined drive has for success are the subjects of considerable discussion. The role that women will play in the business affairs of the future needs to be explored. Women do contribute significantly and efficiently to the progress the business community seeks as its major goal. Today's woman should know why she should view her role in the business drama as being different from that of her male counterpart.

Inasmuch as marketing has also come of age and is increasingly being embraced by more and more of our corporations, today's woman finds her entrance upon the business scene measured in relation to her skills as a marketer. It is those skills and techniques that allow goods and services to reach a marketplace in such a manner as to reap a profit and provide for the future growth and prosperity of the corporation. It is to the development or refinement of these skills for the potential woman executive that this book has directed its focus.

Too much has been made of differences that supposedly exist between men and women and their implications in respect to work accomplishment in the marketing and general business fields. I don't choose to comment extensively on such attitudes other than to say that the collective body of contemporary thought denies these differences, except for equal recognition and compensation for equal work done. The plan for executive achievement which this book will outline proceeds from the premise that men and women are equally well equipped to do whatever job the business sector sets out for them. Having come late to the field of commerce, for a variety of well-known cultural and socioeconomic reasons, a woman finds herself in a catch-up position. She must run hard to assimilate those skills and methodologies neces- sary for superior functioning in the marketing area. She must have a clear understanding from the beginning that the reality of business life is that she will not only have to work harder to reach the same goals as her male counterpart, but that equal recognition, acceptance, and compen- sation will be harder to obtain, although we are seeing marked im- provement in these areas.

Today's marketers are fully aware that their trade is at best an inexact science. Notwithstanding this, there are certain basic principles that have developed and are considered fundamentals. Women must master these fundamentals if they are to be positive assets to the corpora- tion and to themselves. As women professionalize themselves, I feel you'll find that the only differences to surface, those that distinguish them, will be those innovative changes that any new thinking underta- ken by a previously excluded group will make. In the creative marketing area such change will be welcomed; to the extent that it is derivative of female minds now applied to age-old problems in the marketing area, it will make a difference.

If a woman is to be successful, the discipline of her thinking and the development of a set of personal strategies for advancement are primary. Though no firm assurance can be given that adherence to accepted formulas will assure success, it is the experience of many who have arrived that strategies for goal achievement are essential if a realis- tic thrust against an impersonal business world is to be attempted.

Several key and tested personal strategies are outlined herein. They deal with the broader social, psychological, and personal ques- tions that arise with respect to woman's advance in business. An under- standing of these approaches and their strategic implications will be helpful prior to or during the period of your acquisition of the basic marketing skills.

THE LATE START-UP FACTOR

Career planning is fundamental to the upbringing of the American male. The approach is different with respect to the forward planning of many females. For the woman who is already working, the view prior to age thirty often tends toward seeing the work situation as a job—no more, no less. For most, thirty has an almost mystical aura attached to it. For some it is the time of realization that preconceived plans about marriage and childbearing have not materialized, or it can be the time when you recognize you have spent several years tending to family needs and are now prepared to return to the work force. More likely, it is the time you realize that after a few years in the work force you enjoy and want to continue what you are doing. Now you are intent on building a career. Whatever the reason, a transformation in thinking takes place. A conscious effort is made to turn the job into a career.

The impact of marriage and motherhood, more than any other single factor, has generally affected woman's consciousness in such a way as to divert her attention from the long-range plan, the kind of thinking necessary for success in business. Given this particular conditioning, the woman who has made the decision to embark on a business career, at whatever phase of her life cycle, must be more assertive in her pursuit of business knowledge than her male peers. An aggressive attitude toward acquiring those fundamental skills will enable women to cope effectively with male counterparts. Both men and women will be reaching for the largest piece of the corporate pie. For the woman who has not, in her formative years, made the calculated decision to pursue a business career, the knowledge that there is a good deal of catching up to do will be helpful. The determination to forego and make sacrifices in other areas of life is a strategic decision that must be made. It is also vital if you are at all serious about building a career.

THE FEAR FACTOR

Women are actually no more fearful of most things than are men. Women pilot aircraft, serve in armed forces, skydive, perform delicate surgery, give birth to children. They have led revolutions, served behind enemy lines, and charted great expanses of the unknown. Women are conditioned by societal factors to be prone to certain psychological fears, precisely because they are women. In this area, the fear of success looms as a major factor in contributing to the less-than-enviable statistical record of woman's success in business. Inasmuch as woman's lack of self-confidence in the business environment is a result of conditioning, this same conditioning mechanism can be utilized to allay the fear of success and transform the tentative, hesitant woman into a more positive and assertive member of the group. Self-confident men like, respect, and welcome self-confident women. Unfortunately, not all the men that women come into contact with in the work situation feel comfortable initially with the newer, assertive female member of the work team.

These men, who have not yet liberated themselves to the point of thinking in terms of team members rather than female colleagues, will feel threatened by a woman's presence. Given time and a little patience, these men will become aware that the task of achieving business goals requires all the strength and skills that the team can muster. Thus, the woman who has done her homework and is tenacious and aggressive in her pursuit of commonly agreed-upon goals will be more than welcome.

Much current thinking has been brought to bear on the possible loss of femininity that success-oriented women may suffer. There is no woman quite so feminine as the one who is competent and capable. She is the woman who can fully share in the psychological, social, and commercial contract of life.

THE EDUCATION FACTOR

Complexity is the distinguishing characteristic of today's business life. Nowhere is the need for information and skills with which to build, participate in, and manage today's business ventures better recognized than at the corporate management level. The proliferation of business schools, parabusiness institutions of learning, community and business sponsored educational facilities, is graphic testimony to the practical eye with which corporations view those skills necessary for today's managers, tomorrow's business leaders. The woman who sets herself a course of business learning will be ahead of the game. Business demands are such that an almost-instant level of contribution is required of most personnel. For those women who tend toward a more liberal and broader educational base, the task will be harder. The woman who pursues a strategy of tailored education, followed by continuing education, skills will be learned upon which rewards will be readily heaped. New opportunities will quickly open for this woman.

THE "NOBODY GETS A FREE RIDE" FACTOR

The world of business has one overriding dictum that motivates all of its endeavors: Profit is the basic drive. Given this, it seeks to extract from its personnel the maximum levels of performance and efficiency.

The modern corporation seeks as much of its people as it does from the plant and equipment it owns, the capital it shifts from one task to another to insure a maximum return on investment.

Women embarking on a career in marketing will soon recognize that the commitment required will be stringent. Women must be prepared to work hard to achieve a meaningful level of competence. Women will probably have to work harder than their male counterparts because of the residue of the "show me" psychology that still pervades some of the more traditional management.

It is advisable, therefore, to avoid the nine-to-five mentality; and yet, for the sake of one's own self, some balance should be kept. It is no easy assignment, juggling the various demands of career and family. The woman who is prepared to go the extra mile will find that she does no more than does the man seated in the next office.

THE BUSINESS FACTS
OF LIFE

In the business world, the interrelationship of one person to another is of great significance. Business organizations are no more than numbers of people with a single purpose. The business organization hones this assemblage of different personalities, styles, and skills to have it operate as a cohesive unit for the achievement of a commonly shared goal.

Acknowledging this interdependence factor and the true political nature of the business unit can be an eye-opening experience. It can also serve as a first step toward a mature appraisal of those peer group pressures that affect the success ladder the ambitious woman will want to follow.

Two basic rules have stood the test of time and are worthy of adoption for one's personal strategy. First, it is important to recognize that the preponderant benefit to be derived from participation in any business venture is the monetary reward implicit in it. There are lots of things a business is and lots of things that it is not. Business is not a substitute for family. It is not a social haven where work-directed needs are subordinated to personal rewards. What business is, is an agglomeration of humans who all too often will find more to disagree about than to agree upon. The lesson for the astute, aspiring woman executive is that it is not at all necessary to like those persons with whom one is in daily contact. It is, however, imperative that regardless of personal likes and dislikes, an avenue be found so that all persons can work effectively within the environment.

A final aspect of the strategy that can enrich a woman's work life and support her progress is the one that allows her to mature as a businessperson as a result of proper evaluation of the psychological tone of the company for which she will be working. Much like people, companies have a way of either consciously developing or spontaneously assuming distinct personality characteristics. Some are highly aggressive and autocratically dominated. Others assume a lower-keyed approach to problem solving. These latter types are often more contemporary in their thinking and supportive of participatory management undertakings.

Regardless of the type of personality that prevails, the clue to achievement will most often be found in the nurturing of the ever-present *mentor apparatus*. He or she will be obvious to the alert woman. The mentor is the one person in the firm, who, for purely nonselfish reasons, will stand out from the others as a supporter and champion. Often the role is sought out by the mentor as a means to surrogate for some void in his or her own life. The motivation, though, is almost always sincere. The woman who finds herself the recipient of mentor attention can feel that she is blessed. She has been chosen by one who will pave the way for her and guide her through the labyrinth of relationships that are part of every corporation. Mentors are special people. The demands made by them of those whom they guide and protect will only be for the sincere effort to excel.

THE COSMETIC FACTOR

Strategies for career advancement have long since recognized that imagery is an active ingredient in every facet of the business world. Cultivating the proper image is no easy task, but one to which much attention must be paid. It is seldom advisable to attempt a radical alteration of one's personality. The result will be obvious and the façade that is developed will be easily seen through by peers, subordinates, and those higher up.

It's advisable, no matter what one's natural personality type, to maximize presence to whatever extent is in keeping with the real you. This strategy calls for participation, exposure, and a broad attempt to create some awareness of oneself within your particular firm and industry. Remember, executives with low profiles get to keep them! Within the confines of what is comfortable, it is advisable to reach out into activities associated with business that go beyond the everyday work situation. Certain activities which will serve to elevate both one's own self-image and the manner in which others perceive you as a woman executive are participation in trade associations, professional groups, and company/community relation affairs; industry-wide public relations activities such as preparation of articles for trade magazines; and the participation in related seminars, which can provide the opportunity for speaking out on topical issues.

THE "NOTHING VENTURED, NOTHING GAINED" FACTOR

Each and every decision the business woman is called upon to make will incorporate a degree of risk taking. Risk taking as a prudent and well-thought-through strategy is a must for career ascendency. Few people are willing to take these risks, for their capacity to provide opportunity to achieve, as well as to fail, is not too readily grasped.

The conditioning to avoid risk-taking situations and instead to follow the safer avenues is a serious encumbrance which modern woman brings with her to the business world. One of the broader characteristics of contemporary American management style is the caretaker school of management, which seeks only to moderately improve the status quo of the corporation. It devotes its primary energies to activities that are assuredly safe, in that little chance is left for anything negative—or positive—to happen. Against such a background, the challenge-oriented woman will find many difficulties in implementing the new and the innovative. Nonetheless, if women are to make a realistic and creative contribution to the work situation, the pursuit of uncharted waters is mandatory.

For themselves, women will have to be instrumental in eliminating those stereotypical images that have unfortunately attached themselves to all members of their sex. The new, assertive woman will dream a little, remain flexible, learn to listen, sift, diagnose, analyze, and predict. She will take measured steps, yet very real ones, to eliminate the sameness barrier which all too often becomes a standard of executive thinking. She will reach within herself for the entrepreneurial spirit which seeks a different and a better way to do things. She will be what the business organization with an open mind desperately needs—a pragmatic innovator.

Armed, for better or worse, with these guides for personal career development, the enterprising woman will begin to assemble that group of skills which is the armament of the effective marketing executive. I offer a word to you, therefore, about the broader implications of the marketing philosophy as a major movement on the American business scene.

Those dedicated to the marketing way of doing business are still among the minority of business managers. Historically, the primary thrust of the American economic sector has been heavily tilted in the direction of manufacturing whatever the factory was equipped to produce, and only that. Until about thirty years ago, any real appreciation of the influence the consumer had in directing his or her own freedom of choice in the selection of goods and services had been relegated to a backseat.

The distinguishing characteristic of today's marketer is the desire for the enrichment and satisfaction of the consumer, whoever and whatever the profile. The marketer seeks to produce, distribute, and profit from the sale of those goods and services that the consumer indicates it is his or her preference to have made available. Finally, the balance in the American marketplace has shifted in the direction of consumption.

It is the role of the marketer to assemble all those tools available for the profitable satisfaction of this consumer demand. Today's marketer is still a supplier, but only in the most elemental sense of the word. Today's marketer is much more concerned than his or her predecessor with the analysis and assessment of expressed consumer needs as they translate themselves into the production of goods and services that satisfy those needs.

Marketing, as a more efficient approach to the entire area of business and its supply and demand role, appears to be the future approach to our own economic order. It promises to elevate the living standards of millions of Americans and billions of other people around the world. Inasmuch as it is a people-oriented system, its appeal as a career area for woman is, I believe, both obvious and opportunistic.

9

Personal Traits: Career Essentials

The road to a marketing career can begin almost anywhere. Marketers have come from the ranks of journalism, engineering, medicine, law, academia, aviation, and a wide variety of employment backgrounds. An analysis of the characteristics that make for success reveals a certain pattern. In assessing your choice of a career, it is vital for you to review those things that have led you toward deciding on a marketing career. After a careful and honest assessment of key intellectual and character signs that have been identified, a certain feeling of comfort toward the decision you're making will develop. Prior to approaching these specific, predictive characteristics, I will review some observations about marketing as a career based on real world experience.

MYTHS

Myths exist in every career area; marketing has its share. Let me shatter a few specific ones in order to give you a clear perspective. Myth number one is called the uniform myth, that there is a finely defined, special look and demeanor that accompanies the marketer. This, like other of life's stereotypes, is no more than an empty cliché. There are those persons who believe that wearing a specific style of clothing will enable them to fit into the crowd. In every profession there is a uniform look of the masses. If you are truly interested in building a career, you never want to get lost in a crowd or the masses. You want to stand out—not in a freakish manner, but in one that shows you have innate good taste in clothes and appearance, which adds to your image of confidence and success. Put the same thought behind your appearance as you would behind a new product you were introducing to the trade. You want to distinguish it from the competition without alienating your target market. If you need help, there are many publications to refer to, as well as experts in makeup and fashion you can go to for aid. We will be discussing this in further detail in a later chapter.

Number two is the advanced education myth. You don't have to have a parcel of advanced degrees from prestigious institutions of higher learning nicely tucked under your arm in order to make it to the upper business echelons. Yes, a business school education can get you places, but there's nothing quite like on-the-job experience to drive home the most vital lessons you will ever learn. Industry always has a sufficient quota of men and women who are *in theory* fully capable of running million-dollar, even billion-dollar corporations. But theory will never replace practical experience. Meeting budgets, serving customers, handling employee grievances, solving the myriad of day-to-day problems that exist in any business—that is the ultimate test of your abilities. M.B.A.'s and Ph.D.'s aside, practical work experience will be of more benefit in many situations, as will your own personal drives.

Number three is what is referred to as the specialization myth. There is an unfortunate undercurrent and attitude in business circles that seeks to deny the validity of the broad, conceptual mind. Unfortunately, just as much as the marketing skill has developed in response to the need to master the technological processes of production and distribution, this same technological environment has given rise to an overemphasis on what I choose to refer to as mechanics, and an underemphasis on plain old incisive problem-solving thinking. So if yours is the kind of mind that sees a problem and opportunity first in its broad perspective, then don't stumble under the fear of not being able to grasp all the details that go to make up the whole. Strong corporate leadership relies on the ability to see and understand the overall picture rather than just a few segments. Suffice it to say that most businesses can much more readily find mechanics than thinkers. Understand that these myths exist, but they need not be obstacles to your goals.

BUZZWORDS
AND CAREER EVALUATION

As you venture further into your career planning, you will be confronted with an endless stream of words or phrases relating to your capability to fit into a marketing vocation. Here are a few to be aware of, especially when dealing with interviews.

1. Job-type personnel departments would find their work easier if every applicant would easily fall into a particular category. Fortunately, each of us is truly individual, but that doesn't stop people from trying to classify us as research, sales, administrative, or creative types. Try to avoid having a specific label applied to you. You are too complex, and usually the position to be filled is, too.

2. Chemistry. Simply, how will you get along with the others in your department? With luck, you've been developing your human relations skills so this will not be a problem.

3. Team playing. This refers to your capacity to work as part of a group. Surprisingly, those who work well in a team effort often stand out on an individual basis.

4. Promotability. This refers to your potential for advancement.

5. Loner. This classification is not as bad as it sounds, for quite often it is the label assigned to persons who are willing to be their own person, to stick their necks out when they think the firm can benefit from their judgment. If they're right, they benefit as well.

There are many buzzwords in marketing; interviewers often use them to impress you with their skills and power. Don't let them throw you. What you must make sure of is that what you have to offer is known, so it might match the interview criteria for selection, making the interviewer's job and your job easier.

PREDICTING SUCCESS

The best process known for determining success or failure in the marketing field centers upon the following three areas: 1.) personality, 2.) drives, and 3.) special skills. This chapter will devote a good deal of time to the discussion of these factors. Be encouraged by knowing that it is not necessary for you to score yourself an *A* on all of them. If, after careful and honest review, you feel that your overall response is more to the positive than to the negative side of the list, you can feel that your choice of a marketing career will have some reasonable chance for success.

Personality

The tradition is to lump people under convenient labels. This is in keeping with the American mania for order and tidiness, in some cases not an altogether negative trait. In the personality assessment area, much has been made of the so-called distinction between the low-key and the aggressive personality. Inasmuch as people are, in reality, dominated by certain overriding personality characteristics, and yet will and can display other traits running the whole gamut of human emotions, these so-called convenient designations can be misleading if you are rating yourself. Beware of such stereotyping; instead, focus your thinking on what I've come to believe is a workable definition of these two types of persons as it applies to forecasting proper emotional fit within the marketing environment.

The general rule that can be followed is that both the more retiring, less aggressive personality, as well as its outgoing, gregarious counterpart, can find a satisfactory career in the marketing field. It is the proper utilization of personalities within the organization that is the key to making them efficient and productive personnel.

PERSONALITY DEFINED.   Personality, in a technical sense, might be described as the sum total of the physical, mental, emotional, and social characteristics of an individual. More often, one considers it to be the visible aspect of one's character as it impresses others. It should, but does not always, reflect the substance that may lie beneath the exterior. The stereotype of the sales personality as that of an outgoing backslapper has long since gone by the boards. As the world of marketing finds its level of sophistication increasing, it has recognized that some of the greatest sales ever made have been consummated by personality types whose presentation style may indeed have been low-key, even retiring. These persons have somehow learned the lesson that less can definitely be more.

PRODUCTIVE AT A LOW KEY.   If your strong suit lies in getting across the substance, the meat of the matter, then by all means follow your instinct. You'll find that the slick technique that surrounds little substance is rapidly seen through. The situation is reminiscent of theater audiences temporarily dazzled by the method of the performer, but not blinded by these theatrics to the lack of substance of the playwright's message.

The ability to grasp the true meaning of a situation, the need to be fulfilled, the problem to be solved, and the ability to follow through until completion, are all more important traits to those working with you and those you're working for than any showy razzmatazz.

PRODUCTIVE AGGRESSION.   The aggressive personality, oddly enough, can sometimes be benefited most by channeling this distinguishing trait into areas in which aggression could be presumed to be the least useful. The key factor is to use enthusiasm in a productive manner. All too often the so-called aggressive personality type will create irritations, tensions, and general hostility where none is called for. Theirs is the confrontation school of marketing, and the emphasis, unfortunately, is on making the point by bowling the opposition over. Think what wonders of market innovation could be generated if these same energies were directed to more solitary pastimes with fewer opportunities for personal interaction and the subsequent inevitable tensions. The aggressive personality may be best suited to putting passions into the development of written plans, documents, and other disciplined activities.

Once there is a mastery of these energies and they are properly directed, the challenge presented by empty pieces of paper awaiting conversion into words of meaningful communications will be more than enough of a target. As control of the aggressive personality is acquired through such disciplining, it will be a short step thereafter to unleash this tamed and directed aggressive marketer in a more open, person-to-person environment.

It will be obvious, I believe, that this thing we call personality type is a complex undertaking. Inasmuch as self-analysis is a difficult, if not impossible, process, I suggest that if you have any of the normal and healthy hesitancies about your own personality direction, you put the test of your predominant personality type to a close friend or colleague. In an open and friendly exchange, you will most certainly get honest answers.

ON ASSERTIVENESS.   Assertiveness is different from aggressiveness, although the two working in force are more effective in many situations. To be assertive is to act with assurance, confidence, and in a positive manner. The vigorous energy, the forcefulness used in your initiative is the aggressive factor.

Whether you find your own self-tendency either in a low-key or the aggressive direction, the characterisitic of assertiveness will certainly play a role as you ponder the marketing world. This is the quality of simply exercising your will to bring forth those thoughts that you hold with conviction. It is the mind's way of saying it has taken a position on some matter. You have thought it through and what you say or write or do or present can be said to represent what you, in fact, do feel. With no point of view, you cannot hope to move a group, sell an item, or convince a supplier. Your arguments will sound hollow because they are based on nothingness. Assertiveness can make the low-key personality seem like the strongest person in the room. It is a belief in oneself that is bound to affect others. Assertiveness can make an overbearing personality seem less aggressive, for notwithstanding the discomfort the presentation style may bring to an audience, the sincerity of the feelings will win the day.

This discussion of three personality types that populate the marketing field, and your own special fit within the ebb and flow of these human characteristics, should convince you that one of the gospels of this book is that there is no single gospel—no panacea of ideal qualification criteria. Those factors I have discussed will help you determine for yourself those signposts that say this is right or this is wrong for me. As I have found, they are just part of a comprehensive self-examination process which many years of experience indicate is necessary for an honest, face-to-face confrontation with your own future career expectations.

Drives

My own background and experience lead me to discuss this next broad area, which I refer to as Drives. Do you have enough of those key motivations which appear time after time in any character analysis of the successful marketing personality? This list and description of drives may at times run at cross-purposes to your deepest feelings. I am being particularly straightforward when I describe them, for it is the personality—aggressive, low-key, or a blend of the two—who is committed to these drives that will ultimately find success in the world of marketing. Remember, personality is a matter of style. Drives are a much more definitive factor. Either you have drive, and in the degree required, or you don't. Though drives may in time be acquired through the process of education and experience, more than likely the kind of special marketing drives required will be present in you, much like instinct.

Drives result from the sum total of our life experience. Success may be a person's single most important goal in life, resulting from some special psychological need. The environment of your family and friends plays a major role in influencing our drives and their direction. Though human behavior can be restructured through various therapeutic processes, the depth and intensity of drive motivation required for success in the marketing area must be so intense as to come to the marketing world in an almost natural state.

THE PROFIT DRIVE.   In its simplest terms, to profit means to cause an action to take place in which something is exchanged for something of greater value. The difference that accrues to the one who profits can be spent, saved, or invested for additional profit or loss. The fundamental psychology of those who pursue the profit drive is to end up with more than they started with. In the marketing and business world the currencies with which the profit game is most often played are dollars and recognition.

A variety of motivations set the profit drive in motion: greed, financial need, intellect, challenge, ego, sport, chance, and sometimes even charity. The point is that it is more than just simple acquisitiveness that motivates the profit drive. Happily, the drive to profit stems from a variety of causative situations, many of which have positive social benefits. Profit on the whole has a positive social aspect. The profit mechanism works in a circular fashion, benefiting all participants.

Financial profit is what enables businesses to operate, jobs to be available, taxes to be paid, education and the arts to exist, and government to work. Combined with need for emotional profit, it is the basis of our free-enterprise system and, in a sense, our nation.

LEVELS OF DRIVE.   As each individual is totally unique, so is their level of drive. Some have insatiable appetites for material wealth, others for power or fame; and many just have a need to achieve—to be faced with a challenge, meet it head on, and come out a winner. These latter ones are often the motivating forces behind many of the activities that lead to benefits for civilization as a whole. Women in general have tended to be encompassed in the group seeking achievement primarily for achievement's sake.

THE WORK DRIVE.   We hear much these days about so-called workaholics. The term *workaholic* unfortunately has a negative connotation, as it is associated with those who depend on excesses of alcohol. The analogy is ill-founded. For the hard, dedicated worker who recognizes that a person with a nine-to-five mentality might not achieve as much as his or her harder-working counterparts, the workaholic problem is not a problem. If you like and respect the work you do, well, then, you are indeed dependent upon it. And what a happy and constructive habit you've got! The drive to work is one of the most positive forces activating the human personality. Without it, accomplishment dwindles, self-esteem is lost, discovery fades, social progress disappears, and hope takes a backseat to cynicism. You will not always be able to see the fruits of your labor immediately, but one day they will suddenly appear. The pain of what may have seemed excessive hours of unrewarded toil will dissipate in the benefits of accomplishment.

Do not let all this talk about hard work, long hours, pain, endurance, and so on make you lose sight of the fact that smart use of your working hours is more important than the length of your workday. Working at what you enjoy is not work in the sense of what most visualize. Striving for perfection, while knowing it is truly unobtainable, will ensure you a faster climb up the ladder of success.

THE CONCENTRATION DRIVE.   Focusing on one subject to the exclusion of all others is a mental skill that requires a mastery of the fine art of discipline. Combine with this trait the ability to be patient, and the concentration drive comes into focus. If the aspiring marketer is ever to even hope to be successful, it is this ability to concentrate efforts, energies, and the thought process on one particular task that will play a greater role than any other in her march to the top. One must learn the art of concentration. It is a process that allows the mind to push certain extraneous or nonpertinent-for-the-time data to the on-alert areas of the brain. To the forefront are their on-line counterparts. These are the things that you, as marketers, will need to work with at the present moment. They have present-tense utility. They are immediately functional.

HOW TO MASTER CONCENTRATION. Unhappily, the concentration drive will confront many natural enemies in the marketing world. The reality of business life is such that all too much time is required in meetings, memoranda, scheduling, system compliance, and the entire façade of the work world. When all these nonproductive duties are attended to, the time left for concentration is too limited, and the mind often over-inputted with a variety of data extraneous to the matter at hand.

The methods for developing the ability to concentrate vary depending upon which practitioner you talk to. Here are a few of my own.

1. Establish your priorities. Decide what must be achieved first. Preferably take on difficult tasks first. Eliminate the unimportant from your schedule.
2. Eliminate distractions as much as possible.
3. Make yourself and your surroundings as comfortable as possible.
4. Set time limits for the work to be done.
5. Set aside time on a regular basis to review what you're doing and why.
6. Keep yourself organized.

CHOOSE A DESTINATION. Here is one final hint on training the concentration drive to its highest level of performance. It pays to have a mental destination point when summoning your intellect to work at intense levels. Set some goal—for example, a clearly defined stopping point in the preparation of an important report, or an achievement yardstick for a nationwide sales drive, if that is the assignment. By so doing, you will find that you will be narrowing the parameters of the area in which you want to work. This process is an active part of the dynamics of concentration. A succession of such mental destinations will be required along the road to your project's completion.

Once the concentration process becomes an integrated part of the work habit, it will come more easily. The momentum generated will simplify the effort. Destination points will be further and further apart and yet will be achieved more easily. Concentration is a discipline that reinforces itself through conditioning. Don't shy away from it. If you master the concentration drive, you may well open up a whole new world for yourself.

THE POLITICAL DRIVE.   When profits, achievement, and progress are involved in any process, and all are present in the marketing world, one is certain to find the political drive in action. It is a required force for the woman whose ultimate goal is the top of the ladder. By the rules of the political drive, there will be those who win and the less fortunate who may drop by the wayside. The political drive transcends basic skills. Often it has nothing whatsoever to do with competence. It is capricious, subjective, and not always fair to the people involved or rewarding to the corporation's stated objectives.

COPING WITH POLITICS.   There is no one school of thought to comfort aspiring marketers with easy rules for handling the political drive. If yours is the type of personality that takes naturally to politicizing every aspect of the work situation, then your best avenue to success may lie in this direction. If, on the other hand, you have strong motivation to let your ideas and actions speak for themselves, then this direction should be followed. Marketers, whatever their personal preferences, need to be ever mindful of those very active political drives that will most certainly be working among colleagues. Politics is a fact of life in every business situation. Obviously, the larger the firm, the greater the proportion of political activity. Knowing that this factor exists, and admitting to yourself that to some degree it always will, lends credence to a commonsense decision to sharpen your own political drive. It is realistic to learn how to deal with this. If the greater part of work activity is based on what one considers to be the merits of the case, then the political considerations will not weigh so heavily, especially if you've learned to handle them.

THE COMPETITIVE DRIVE.   Of all those driving forces that are vital to success in the marketing field, probably none occupies as wide an area of interest and attracts so much discussion as does the competitive drive. The reason is obvious. The give-and-take within the free enterprise system has been so successful that the institutionalization of competition, which is at its core, has led to a standard of living unmatched in any other form of government. At the heart of the competitive drive seen in America is a dimension that is easily identified amongst those personalities who occupy positions of leadership in the marketing sector. This trait is the ability to act and react in a manner that seeks to find a better way to make or do something. This drive separates the men from the boys, the girls from the women. There are winners and losers along the way. But society in general is better off because competition has taken place.

CONTROLLING COMPETITION

In the business world, the channeling of competitive drives can help to make or break careers. Endless competitive activity within the organization can be devastating to the intended purpose for which any one particular business unit has been brought together. On the other hand, the kind of competitive environment in which executives are urged to do better than the friend who may sit in the next office can be beneficial if the competitive ground rules acknowledge that the prize will be one of recognition and status as a professional. This type of competitive environment affirms that it is important for every member of the marketing group to compete and contribute to his or her utmost. It further recognizes the necessity for every member of the group to at one time or another share the sweet success that comes with a business victory.

To Compete or Not

If you're building a career, the answer is obvious. Not to compete is just the same as saying you wouldn't strive to do your best. Some women shy from the competitive atmosphere, as do some men. If you feel this is a problem area, then it is best to recognize it early in your career. Not only will women be expected to compete within the organization, but the very foundation of marketing sits at the center of the world's most competitive environment—business. If one is willing and able to come to terms with these rules of the game, opportunities will come, as well as enjoyment in the competition.

Special Skills

I believe it's wise to find those areas or skills within oneself which are unusually well-developed. After noting them, it is desirable to be in a position within the organization that allows for the display and utilization of these special skills. Chances are that though a woman may take second or even third place in any given list of ten different job performance areas, there will be one special area where she will come out on top. Concentration in this area can be rewarding, for it can reap victories—and, in some cases, in a noncombative manner. Special skills are not readily or easily come by. If a person possesses one or several skills that they perform better than most competitive members of the group, the group will grudgingly acknowledge this person's superiority. Competitors won't suffer for, after all, they can't expect to win every time. Colleagues will have to do with a shorter list of conquests, and happily, everyone comes out ahead.

CHARACTERISTICS

There are many characteristics important to marketing, but three that should be highlighted are analysis, vision, and creativity. They are difficult to learn, as most come in an inherent manner, but if you have a seed of any or all, cultivate it.

Analysis

The first of these characteristics is the power to analyze. The mind of the marketer must be able to see the implications of a large number of different and seemingly unrelated facts. The marketer must be able to cut through the layers and layers of data and cull out what is relevant. That is the first step of analysis: finding the tools with which to work. From this data, the analytically oriented marketer must be able to define the problem. What do the facts of any business situation indicate has to be done? Is the company's future growth dependent on its product, knowing the competition, apparent financial restrictions on growth, or what have you? It is only after a proper analysis of the problems has been made that the search for solutions can begin.

Vision

What will be the effect of today's marketing actions on the future? The mere ability to think in terms of a tomorrow is the surest clue available to that special skill that is vision. Companies grow, companies and markets and their products and customers change. Markets change. The kind of mind that will understand the broad ramifications of such a seemingly innocent action as price change is the kind of mind the marketing world looks for. Will the marketer's mind recognize that the establishment of one successful brand in the marketplace may justify an unusually high cost of initial expenditure, providing this brand lends itself to additional subsequent sizes? This is the classic line-extension theory of marketing. Will the marketer's mind recognize the value of capital expenditure, to be ready ten years hence for the penetration of markets that don't currently exist? This is the kind of thinking that gave birth to the Xerox copying machine, a successful effort to manage the data explosion. These are the vision traits that all senior executives in the marketing field possess. They will surely look for them in you. These are the special skills that allow one to be put on the list of growth candidates for the management teams of tomorrow.

Creativity:
The Power of Imagination

A word about the creative process. This, too, is a special skill, and yet it is more than this. Of the three—analysis, vision, and creativity—the last is the hardest to put one's finger on. The creative process has been studied for years in an effort to be able to reproduce its workings. The hope is to make each and every being more creative. The results, in this experiment, are far from encouraging. There would seem to be no single set of rules that can guarantee the one thing that makes the marketing world— indeed, the entire business world—go around. No one has found the formula for manufacturing an idea. The woman who is creative and can make an original contribution to the marketing environment need only count her blessings.

I suggest you do not try to understand your own creative processes. To analyze them is to formalize, hinder, and restrict them. But it is a skill that can be nurtured, upgraded, and sharpened.

FOOD FOR THOUGHT

Following is a thought-provoking quiz with a unique twist. You should take it twice—now and when you have finished this book. Save your answers and compare. You may be surprised at how your responses may change.

1. In developing a sales presentation, what should be my first consideration?
a. Highlighting the product's features. b. Detailing the profit potential that can be generated. c. Defining the problem/need.

2. Given a limited advertising budget, I would:
a. Segment my marketing direction. b. Compete with the brand leaders. c. Spend on trade promotion, not advertising.

3. Learning to manage my time is:

a. A matter of common sense. b. Good discipline. c. A necessary management technique.

4.   Work experience is considered valuable because it:
a. Increases one's efficiency. b. Sharpens one's skills. c. Broadens one's perspective.

5.   One's morning office procedure should start with:
a. Making all important phone calls. b. Opening mail; setting day's priorities. c. Scheduling day and meetings.

6.   I would define a career as:
a. A life-style. b. A financially rewarding job. c. An opportunity that depends on skill.

7.   How would I describe a philosophy of "all work and no (or little) play" in building a career?
a. Highly productive. b. Detrimental. c. Necessary in the early stages of career building.

8.   Testing is a marketing tool designed to reduce risk and financial disaster. Should I:
a. Make it a rule in all situations. b. Do it only in high-risk situations. c. Judge each situation separately.

9.   When I have what I feel is a new or strong idea, I:
a. Write it down. b. Place it in the back of the mind for future reference. c. Act on it immediately.

10.   In writing a marketing plan, my first step would be to:
a. Reread the previous plan. b. Meet with other concerned departments for their thoughts. c. Outline all my thoughts.

11.   Which do I consider will be my most valuable skill as a marketing executive?
a. Thorough knowledge of marketing techniques. b. Ability to motivate and communicate with others. c. Ability to keep an open mind.

12.   In developing marketing strategies, I:
a. Always follow the same approach. b. Watch the competition closely. c. Keep an open mind.

13.   Which do I think best describes the profitable direction of the future?
a. Bigger and better. b. Better but not bigger. c. Smaller, segmented service.

14.   The wave of the future will be:
a. More products. b. Different products. c. Special-interest products.

15.   Leadership can be:
a. Taught in graduate schools. b. Developed through practical experience. c. Experienced by anyone.

16.   The marketing department is:

a. A sum of its various parts. b. The focal point of the corporation. c. Dependent upon all the other departments.

If you thought that in some questions all the answers were appropriate, you were probably right . . . maybe. The business world is not one of black or white, but many, many shades of gray.

10

Career Entry Levels: Where to Start

Long before the last strains of the dear old alma mater have faded away, the aspiring marketer will be facing the practical matter of how to put a considerable store of hard-earned knowledge to work. Though the educational process many readers are currently completing will have far more than the obvious financial benefits as an end objective, I think it is realistic to assume that some assistance is in order to narrow down those choices of job opportunity that can help in career achievement in marketing.

Today's marketing organizations are increasingly faced with attitudes from all sectors of society that emphasize the life-gratifying or psychological aspects inherent in the manufacture and movement of goods and services. A product is no longer just a simple artifact. Its presence and purchase may well reflect a coming together of factors as wide-ranging as ecology, world political situation, growth or decline of a demographic category, labor situation, new technology, convenience, the Puritan ethic, even the tenets of hedonism. The point I am making is that a well-informed society is forever questioning those issues that surround the statements made by the products or services we have available to us. And the marketer operating in this new environment must have different skills than her predecessors.

Primary to these new skill requirements, two abilities are needed: the ability to be aware of change and the ability to handle it. I call this being informed, and cannot emphasize enough the need to read trade publications, business publications, and so on, and placing oneself in a position that allows for maximum access to the source of change—people.

If you are seriously considering a career in marketing, and excepting those persons whose advance degrees may well place them directly into corporate marketing environments such as the brand management field, be aware that there are certain key entry-level career opportunities which by the nature of the job function give the aspiring marketing manager greater access to these new primary skills than do others. Three have been chosen as a result of a review of the successful careers of several of today's top-level marketers. They are advertising, personal selling, and sales promotion.

Each of these entry-level occupations touches on those key factors I've previously reviewed in arriving at a realistic definition of this thing called marketing. Each involves product, pricing, distribution, advertising, and the sales promotion function, as well as market research and public relations. Though not all of these entry-level career areas will provide an in-depth relationship with all of the elements in the marketing mix, enough will be there for the reader to grasp the essence of the larger picture. Some will be more helpful than others in that they will add the required dimension of being able to see and evaluate the nuances of the interrelationships of the various factors. All will lead the reader to think of the primary need of the marketer to forge a path between the product and the satisfaction of consumer needs. All will provide access to the original thinking of the people who shape our products and services and to the sometimes contradictory, sometime arbitrary, sometime logical, sometimes enigmatic and always fast-changing nature of their thought processes.

ADVERTISING

Entering the marketing world through the field of advertising is an ideal way to get your feet wet. This profession, which has such an important effect on our daily lives, was invented by people who, in the modern sense, saw advertising as a logical extension of personal salesmanship. Faced with an explosion in the number of goods and services spewing forth from America's technological arsenal, they sought some cost-efficient manner of getting the selling message to large numbers of people. From the very beginning, advertising focused on people. Its main task was and is to persuade people. As such, it will offer women marketers a close look at and feel for what motivates the consumer.

It is important to say at the outset that advertising concerns itself with attitudes of different types of consumers and with many different consuming groups, some of which are professionals; housewives; business, industrial, technical, government, and institutional personnel; and many more.

Central to the operation of the advertising process and the foundation upon which most advertising agencies or company advertising departments are structured are the following key functional areas, which together make up the advertising process: media, creative, and account management. Each will be dealt with separately, and you will soon see how a concern and appreciation for the people and change process inherent in the marketing philosophy comes into play.

Entry-level trainees at most large American advertising agencies, large or small, more often than not find themselves toiling in what is referred to as the media department. This experience quickly sheds light on the thousands of ways a modern economy has invented for delivering to people what is hoped will be messages of persuasion. In general, broad media vehicles break down into three categories: print, broadcast, and outdoor media. The latter is defined as the entire area of signage, ranging from highway billboards to railroad stations and airport neon spectaculars.

As a media trainee, you will soon find yourself busily involved in dissecting the relative merits of one medium over another. Each medium has things that it is better suited to do than the next. Each, as a beginning, expresses its persuasive capability and its ability to help the advertiser make his marketing actions efficient and effective by the measurement of circulation. What is measured is the numerical impact of the media. The second dimension that the media trainee will become familiar with is the nature and composition of these faceless numbers. The art of demography delineates the living, breathing persons behind the numbers. With advertising efficiency a costly ingredient in the marketing mix, this does make a difference. Demography counts people on the basis of sex, age, geography, income, color, occupation, city, and size of residence. People can be studied as to their past purchasing preferences and their reading, viewing, or listening habits. They can be analyzed and codified on a heavy, light, and nonuser basis.

They can be further dissected with respect to the relative costs of reaching them. The media trainee will soon be able to convert the statistical picture into the advertising skill of media analysis. The major facts of life will become obvious. Circulation and the study of circulation demography will build a picture of people. Knowing how to reach them is a primary step in the process of knowing how to persuade them. A portrait of just who and how many there are will be extremely helpful to the marketer who is planning an effective strategy of persuasion.

If you are fortunate, your advertising job training will carry you through an apprenticeship in the creative department. Though you may not find yourself able to compose one single line of successful selling copy, the experience will be worthwhile. The creative process in the world of advertising concentrates its energies on people, also. Here the trainee will become aware of those things that move people and motivate them in such a manner as to bring about the desired result for the advertiser. The creative process constantly probes the innermost thinking of those people it hopes to affect, and the world of advertising applies many sophisticated research techniques to do this.

Creators will want to know what consumers think; what governments need in their role as purchasers of goods and services; what the consensus is in a four-person household with respect to the size, color, horsepower, and pollutant emission rate of the new car models. Creators will want to be aware of what the competition is doing, what the most sought-after fall fashion color is, and what the top corporate management of a major multinational client sees as its role in the private sector. Does the corporation feel it is important to display a business ethic, or will the impact of management's thinking be directed to profits at any cost? The corporate advertising campaign of the Sperry Rand Corporation, which admonishes people to train workers in the art of effective listening so as to improve communication and productivity, is an excellent example of a responsible corporate advertising philosophy.

If you as an aspiring marketer are doing your homework, you will readily see the marvelous opportunity that exists for you. The persuasive art of advertising requires—yes, demands—access to people's innermost thoughts and feelings. Nowhere will you daily see so many point of views, sometimes—oftentimes—conflicting. Nowhere will you find such rapid change. Today's slim jeans become tomorrow's billowing pants.

Presumably if that management is on top of change, it will incorporate the new look into part of its line. Nowhere, if you are astute, will you be able to test your evaluation of what these changing attitudes mean as readily as you will in the single area of advertising where the process of persuasion is distilled.

There is an adage that has long since been proven a truism in the world of the advertising agency creative department: "The last thing to be done is to put pencil to paper." I suggest you pay heed to it. With so much marketing data, such a profusion of input about various consuming groups to be gathered, digested, and analyzed, the value of being informed will be obvious. Make certain you are informed before you test your creative prowess.

The final area that your training will take you through is the area known as account management. Less specialized than the others, it, more than media or creative, most closely approximates the skills the true marketer brings to her profession.

The account manager's vision and training must be broad enough to allow her to bring together all the parts of the advertising process and direct them in such a way that they function effectively in the role assigned to advertising in the market mix.

Added to this job requirement are other important tasks. The account manager also assumes the important role of business consultant to the client as well as salesperson for the agency's wares. All the bucks stop at the account manager's desk. She will be on the firing line daily.

In her position she will have to master not only those skills of the advertising process, but also those skills of the marketer. In an efficiently operating advertising agency-client relationship the account manager will know almost as much of the detail, strategies, and objectives of the client's business as does the client. Total immersion is required. The responsibility of the account manager will be to assimilate the marketing data, analyze the problems and the opportunities, and then bring all these marketing weapons that advertising has to offer to the task of persuading. The account manager will have to translate her client's objectives into language that has meaning for her own creative and media personnel. The account manager will have to set the course of her personnel on a straight line toward solving problems that arise from the people nature of her client's business.

PERSONAL SELLING

The field of personal selling, for years closed to women, is the newest, most dynamic, and perhaps most opportunity-oriented entry-level job situation. Selling is a profession requiring a high degree of communication skills and a constant polishing and expanding of those skills. The character traits of charm, warmth, credibility, and persuasiveness, which have so long been directed by women to matters of the home, can be easily adapted to the environment that will be met in the selling situation.

As a preparatory step for your career as a marketer, personal selling will give you daily contact with real people in real situations, reacting or not reacting as a result of a thousand and one influences, each of which can affect their moods, their attitudes, and their decision-making processes. Once you are out there, you're in a position to see changing people and developing points of view as they occur.

Selling is a very personal profession; thus, there are as many different ways to skin a cat as there are cats. There are schools of thought that call upon heavily structured presentations. First you are to do this, then—and only then—you are to do that. I for one have long since abandoned this structure. Professional selling is also an art, and the key to the art is to sell yourself. Yes, oddly enough, the product or service you are selling should come last in your hierarchy of things to do in order to make the sale.

A selling situation is essentially one that centers upon the matter of need. Purchasers must have needs, real or perceived, if anything is to happen. Assuming there is some need that has been expressed by the person to whom you are directing all your persuasive power, the problem then becomes one of satisfying this need in the most pleasurable manner possible. I am not being coy, and I don't want you to be naive.

Chances are that most items of service you may be called upon to sell will have many competitors. Unless you are fortunate enough to represent a company with a one-of-a-kind product, your competitor may well be sitting on the seat next to yours in the waiting room. In filling your prospective customer's needs, he must be convinced not only that your product or service will satisfy a specific need, but you must be convincing enough to persuade that only your relationship as purveyor of this product can assure that his many other needs will be satisfied also.

And what are these needs that separate those women who get the business from those who don't? They go under many names: professionalism, competence, businesslike manner. What I think they really are is something women are quite adept at. You will have to give your customer a feeling of comfort, reliability, peace of mind, and, importantly, make him or her feel that rather than having just been sold something, they have instead chosen to buy—and from you!

Now this piece of advice may seem contradictory. Why should you focus your energies on what appears to be only the psychological aspects of selling? Simple. Selling is a psychological process. Most people you will call upon have been schooled in a purchasing environment that acknowledges the buyer-beware attitude. And probably for good reason. Let me be honest. Many a sale has been made that was unwarranted, ill-conceived, poorly followed up. These are the sales that plague marketers long after profits have been reaped. An ill-wrought sale can do immeasurable damage to a good product because it undercuts the repeat sale, a must for market success.

Purchasers have been the subject of too much high pressure. They now have their defensive barriers up. You will have to knock these walls down before you can even begin to get to what I refer to as the center of the selling situation, probing the specific needs and presenting your product's merits with respect to fulfilling these needs. So getting your prospect to the point at which he or she will be listening to and hearing you is all-important. You know it is a selling situation and the prospect knows it is a selling situation, and that can spell discomfort.

I suggest you do everything but explicitly sell. Try to get the customer to open up. Try to have him or her talk about his business. Shift the focus of the conversation from you and your product to the problem or need. Try to strike a responsive chord. See if anything in your experience can indicate to your customer that you see things from their point of view. At all costs, avoid labeling your meeting as one in which there are two clearly defined sides, the customer and the salesperson. Then, and only then, begin to turn the conversation to specifics. Present your credentials and convince the buyer of your interest in him or her. Then, if you are not by that time invited to do so, ask if you may be allowed to present your wares. And herein lies the crux of the getting-close-to-people problem. Your product may have the most advanced list of features and capabilities in its category. It may be the best-priced, the most dependable, and the most reliable. But unless you have been astute enough in your preliminary conversations to establish an open and honest rapport with your customer, you will be unable to evaluate how your product fits the needs of your prospect.

Do you, for instance, understand how it will be used? Do you recognize how important your product is in the long list of things that your prospect has on the purchasing list? Is yours an important product from that point of view? Can the right purchase make your customer look able and important in the eyes of his peers and superiors? And, by the way, what homework have you done to show him that you care about his business and are not just there to make a sale? Have you, for example, read his company's annual report? If you've been smart enough to do so, you might find out that his division has led the company in sales and profits for the year. You might be in a selling situation with the next divisional manager. A little compliment can go a long way. Don't think of your sales call as an isolated incident. Instead, think of it as the start of what may be a long-term relationship.

Above all, remember the cardinal rule of selling: *Ask for the order.* Don't hesitate, and if you don't get it, try to assess why you failed. In closing the sale, it's vital to know if and when you have gotten to the point of asking the key question. After several minutes in your prospect's office, your own good common sense will tell you if you have made a connection. Trust your instincts. If you have connected, then say something as simple as, "That's the story I came here to fill you in on. Now if I can do anything for you, I'd be happy to." The prospect will know he is being asked for an action response. The answer can come in a variety of fashions. A flat no, a maybe, or an avoidance of the situation.

The magic words that will make your spirits soar, "I'll take a carload," are rarely heard. If the prospect won't commit immediately, be on the lookout for what I call the "leave it open" options. If you're asked to call back or send more material, then you have scored your initial victory. The prospect is indicating that for whatever her or his reasons, a commitment cannot be made on the spot. Don't let it get to you! The door has been left open and most likely you can still get that order. Remember, objections raised are the prospect's way of saying, "I want to buy from you . . . if you can deliver what you say."

Personal selling is a long-term process. As in any personal relationship, there is a beginning, a middle, and an end. If you want your sales experience to be a productive and rewarding one, make certain you've got the patience and tenacity to see the process through in each of its three stages.

Now, some personal thoughts about the opportunities that sales presents as an opening wedge and a training ground for marketers. As I have already noted, being out there on the firing line will give you constant access to vital components of marketing, what the people are thinking, and the nature of coping with change. These factors have direct application to marketers' skills. Multiply the elusive customers you will be calling upon by the millions who may make up a consumer purchasing group, and you have a market; transfer the knowledge you have gained of one specific person to what you think are the needs of a large number of people, and you begin to have the makings of strategic thinking. Take the care and feeding that has gone into selling yourself first, the product second, and apply this same approach to the mood in which your advertising agency will set its upcoming television commercial, and you'll have achieved the highly desirable goal of having the viewing public like your advertising.

Each of the lessons I am pointing out will and do have specific relation to your long-sought marketing career. They will be invaluable, essentially because you will have been out there in the real world.

A final, personal note about sales. In no area of the business and marketing world has entrance into a career area been as difficult for women as in the area of sales. As a woman, I am proud to see the achievement of other women, many of whom are now making it. I believe it will give women further opportunity to develop those assertive characteristics that will be required of them. In certain areas it will undoubtedly bring women into the heart of the process of selling products that they, more than men, are concerned, capable, and more expert with. And for the corporation that has been wise enough to put women on the road side by side with her male colleagues, the bottom-line results are becoming the envy of the competition.

SALES PROMOTION

Because it is hard to conveniently classify, and because in broad, general terms it is less visible and less glamorous than is the advertising function, this entry-level career opportunity is too often overlooked when one thinks of ways to penetrate the marketing world. Sales promotion is being recognized now for the key role it plays. Advertising makes the consumer aware of the product's existence; sales promotion gets the consumer into the store to buy.

My own experience has shown sales promotion to be one of the most important links in the marketing process. And as such, the sales promotion discipline trains the aspiring marketer in a host of skills that will be called upon in most marketing jobs. Let me point out that in the area of access to people and in the skills of managing and being aware of change, the sales promotion field has few peers.

Let me start out by trying to take a leaf from my own experience and tell you how sales promotion should be defined. It is a two-step process focusing on marketing activities that go to aid the sell-in process—getting the product or service into distribution, and secondly, the sell-through process—moving something into the hands of some specific group. I should point out that many of those techniques used in the sell-in process are identical to those used in the sell-through process. It is only the audience that will be affected and will change.

Another factor I believe may help in avoiding confusion with respect to distinguishing sales promotion from its sister marketing activity, advertising, is what I call the "who is the star" factor. When you get involved with sales promotion activities, they will most often concentrate on something that is happening around or surrounding the product. In the more traditional advertising area, what is focused on is the product itself. Sales promotion can be viewed as an activity that adds something to the product or service about which the communication effort centers, so as to make the sale.

Other factors should be kept in mind. Those activities that make up the sales promotion function are usually limited in duration. Inasmuch as they are conceived to add an additional dimension, they are usually nonrecurring in nature during the major cycle of any one marketing period.

The sales promotion function will contribute significantly to your ability to grasp the subtleties of the interrelationship of product, pricing, distribution, advertising, sales promotion, market research, and public relations, which together make up the marketer's mix of activities. It is precisely because the role of sales promotion is to add an extra dimension to the product or service being communicated that it has such value for the future marketer. For the added benefit that sales promotion brings to the marketing process to be effective, it must complement all the other activities undertaken in the marketing mix. The management of change which sales promotion skills add to is a function you will most certainly be called upon to master.

Typical examples of sales promotion activities, either sell-in or sell-through, will graphically drive home the picture of its utility. When the mailman delivers a 1.5-ounce sample of a new shampoo, housed in a gray box, with a plain label marked "Occupant," that is an example of sampling. It is a tried-and-true new-product-introduction technique. In order to properly match your sample delivery with that recipient who you think may be most likely to purchase the full size when she sees it on her supermarket shelf, you will undoubtedly be involved in the process of demographic study of occupant mailing lists. As you see, it keeps getting back to people.

If, prior to launching a new airline package to the Orient (the kind Japan Airlines and Pan American use consistently), you have been wise enough to prepare a brochure that will alert travel agents to the benefits of special incentives, free vacation trips (which can be made available to their sales personnel if they enter a salesman's incentive program and end up at the top of the sales achievement ladder), then you will be involved in a classic experience in the area of personal motivation. What changes people, and how can you get the low-level achievers to rise to greater heights? Dangle a free vacation in front of them, and not only will your sales promotion technique be effecting change, it will also be controlling it.

Sales promotion takes many forms: displays, coupons redeemable for cash, contests offering valuable prizes, trade show exhibits complete with product literature, plant tours, and the like. All are effective in creating positive attitudes about products or services. All have the extra benefit of being immediately measurable. In other words, unlike its less-specific marketing tools such as advertising and public relations, the sales promotion function can be held to quick accountability. A cost-efficiency index can be put to this activity to determine very quickly if the dollars invested have paid out.

As I contemplate these three overviews of career opportunities that lead to a marketing career, let me emphasize my belief that they are in no sense the only avenues open to you. Retailing and market research definitely are entry-level job opportunities. The three I have outlined will be most valuable, though, because at one time or another they will most probably make you stop and think about how their implementation affects all the other elements in the marketing mix. Once you see this interrelationship, you will certainly realize that no one function is a marketing island. Knowing this, your climb to much broader areas of marketing responsibility should be an easier one.

11

Sooner or Later You're Going to Write a Plan

Plans preparation and presentation has made as well as aborted many marketing careers in the making. More than any other skill involved in the marketer's capacity, this is the one I feel is responsible for the greatest amount of difficulty aspiring marketers will face. Whether it is the writing, conception, understanding of the function, or just what group of circumstances places such strain on the plans-preparation function, suffice it to say it is a skill that can and should be mastered. Let me assure you it is not an impossible task. However, as in any area, you can benefit from the experience of others.

My first exposure to plans came at an early stage in my career. I have since been through the short form, and long form, the so-called bible techniques, the evaluate-them-by-the-pound era, as well as the main book and so-called data-back-up-book technique. One thing that has been driven home to me as a result of this experience is that too often the purpose for which planning is done is lost in the process of plan development.

The cardinal rule of plans preparation, which I suggest to you as a good one to follow, is that before you commit the first word to paper, you should sit back and take a long, hard look at why you are about to write this document. If you allow yourself the time to ponder the plan's utility, why you are preparing it, who it is to be directed at, you will be correctly positioning your thinking for the accomplishment of your communications task. And that, of course, is what plans preparation is all about—communicating. A marketing plan is a communications document whose main purpose is to serve as a guideline for the readers, giving a clear-cut idea as to what the company's course of action should be with respect to any particular aspect of its business. We will center upon the concept of planning per se and just how the written document we refer to as a plan fits into the scheme of things.

Marketing plans are the natural by-product of a process known as strategic planning. The nature of this process is long-range, though sometimes the technique can be modified and utilized for shorter-duration planning. The concept of strategic planning is to think about the future of your business and to be ready for it. In the process, you will have accumulated considerable data upon which to draw conclusions and subsequently take action. Thus the process actually has two distinct phases: planning and implementation. When this process is applied to activity in the marketing area, then we come up with the marketing plan. Nothing in the concept has changed but the title. All the implications of strategic planning are included.

Any individual who has just come to the marketing world may have difficulty in understanding the marketing plan and its preparation because their experience is limited. In most corporations with which I have been associated, plans preparation is a group effort. Usually the activity is chaired by a midlevel market manager who will have several years of experience working on a brand or special service or product. As new marketers, you will probably be called upon to contribute, either in the collection of data, in its evaluation, or, in some cases, in the actual planning process itself. Whatever your level of responsibility, an understanding of the purpose of the plan and some insight into how to prepare and write one will certainly make your life and your career progress a good deal easier.

A marketing plan is the marketer's way of placing her thoughts on achievement into one written source. It is a way of seeing that the profit and growth course of a business is committed to and acted upon. It is available in order to make direction as specific as possible for all participating members of the business organization.

Inasmuch as the marketing plan is the business document that gets a foundation for the company's other operating plans to be built, you must have an understanding of all factors that will affect the performance of a business. Remember that the goals, principles, procedures, and methods that will determine the success of your firm's or your product area's future are integrated into the marketing plan.

Though your experience in the business world is at first limited, your education should provide you those basics necessary for a minimal understanding of the factors in and the general objectives of any marketing plan. Obviously, as a communication tool, the marketing plan must integrate all elements of the marketing mix into one comprehensive program for all levels. That includes advertising, sales, public relations, promotion, and much more. Plus, the plan allows the company to make better use of its resources, unify effects, designate responsibilities and schedules, identify problems to overcome and opportunities to take advantage of, control and evaluate all activities, and so on. Once you begin to grasp this big picture, your comprehension of the dynamics of the planning procedure will take place. For you will see that it is a logical process which depends on adherence to doing things in a prescribed sequence: Planning will come first, and then implementation.

There are several tried-and-true formats and disciplines that can be adhered to in the preparation of marketing plans. My experience indicates that they fall into two main categories: separating the planning and implementing sections, or combining the two. My own preference is for the first method. It has the advantage of directing the reader's thoughts more closely to the big picture. I feel it is necessary for the marketer who is affected by a plans thrust of considerable importance to have the time to ponder this big picture. This perspective must be available prior to the time she is asked to assess and/or carry out the implementation activities called for as a result of the market demands of the big picture. For today's well-prepared, well-informed marketing executive, I feel it is unjust to combine execution data with planning data in one sequence. This has the effect of rendering the level of discussions with respect to the strategies proposed. If you are asked to pass judgment and to do something when you may still be wondering whether it should be done, the marketing world is not giving you the opportunity to respond with your best foot forward.

There is an additional reason for my preference of the planning-implementation sequence. Marketing managers will find soon enough that the nature of their job is such that most of their time will be devoted to action activities. You will be deciding on or taking action most of the time. There will be precious little time to sit back and think. If in the activity of plans preparations you continue this emphasis on execution, you will compound the problems that arise as a result of lack of time to make evaluations. The penalty to your executive skill development will be severe. As you move up the ladder, the skills required for senior marketing positions will stress your ability to think. It is preferable to practice the sequencing of your thinking early in your career. Even though plans preparation may only occupy a month or two of any one marketing year, the disciplines of sequential thinking which you will learn will be of value.

In order to make plans preparation more easily understood, I have reviewed dozens of plans prepared by several different companies. As I read them, one principle factor became obvious. A standardized set of definitions is required if plans preparation is to be executed properly. What I mean is that there is a good deal of misuse and misunderstanding of words. Obviously, any person writing anything will bring to the task the cumulative effects of his or her own linguistic prejudices. As a matter of fact, I'm certain that the same can be said for those definitions I utilize in this book. Nonetheless, it is important to attempt a clarification of the terms.

In the following few pages I will try to reduce the margin of error for you. The best way I can think of to do this is to review and define the key areas you will have to cover in plans preparation. You can and, I hope, will consider them a broad format to be followed in the preparation of the plans you will be involved with. Let me state quite firmly that barring highly unusual circumstances, this format should work for you. If your career does involve the interaction of the five key points that make up the market—product/service, pricing, distribution, advertising, and sales promotion—then regardless of the nature of the business you are in, you should be able to utilize this format. Naturally, some of the detail required, especially when I am speaking about qualitative data, will vary, but the essential thrusts of the format should see you through. Most important are the four principles of writing any marketing plan.

1. Communicate in simple, easy-to-understand language.
2. Be precise. Detail clearly to eliminate misunderstandings.
3. Don't be unrealistic. Be practical in achievement of goals and methods utilized.
4. Be adaptable, flexible to the need for change, if necessary.

As I noted earlier, my preference is for starting off with the planning section, so let's take a look at its critical parts.

PLANNING

Direction

In developing the marketing plan, be it for the company, a division, or a single product, you must take into consideration the direction given by top management for the company as a whole.

That direction will encompass three basic questions:

1. What business are we in?
2. What additional business do we wish to enter?
3. What are the markets we should be addressing?

Obviously, growth will have to refer to those areas with the best profit growth and consistent with existing or planned company resources—human, material, and financial, in order to reach your goals.

Goals

Whenever feasible, goals should be in measurable terms so you can see your progress. They should be realistic, so they can be attained, but high enough so the attainment is not too easy.

FINANCIAL GOALS.   These goals are specific and can be short- or long-range, such as:

> Profit
> Sales volume
> Sales growth
> Return on sales
> Return on investment
> Return on assets
> Earnings per share of common stock
> Working capital
> Inventory control
> Backlog of orders

NONFINANCIAL GOALS.   These goals are equally important:

> Corporate and product image
> Share of market

In creating your plan, be sure you designate who has responsibility for what activity. Try to schedule due dates for all aspects of the programming. Simply stated, to ensure that a plan will work, make sure of three things:

1. It is organized.
2. It is organized.
3. It is organized.

Situation Analysis

This is the section that will supply you with the facts needed for planning. It will have the effect of giving a background of the business situation. Its purpose is to provide a frame of reference to guide your thinking. If, for example, your marketing efforts are being devoted to a brand that has already been introduced and is about to enter its second year of market activity, a review of accomplishment problems, competition, and so on to date will be invaluable. The situation analysis can draw a concise picture of sales and profit performance, indicate where the product or service stands with respect to strategies intended to sell the product, or evaluate the progress of a program against established norms for similar programs. The situational analysis should also comment on any radical changes in the product's prescribed marketing course, and, in broad general terms, set the stage for any possible change in direction. It will be invaluable to most marketing organizations in which personnel changes and shifting assignments are a reality that must be faced. It should be prepared in a forthright manner, with as full a disclosure of the facts as is possible.

A good guide for the preparation of an effective situational analysis is to treat it as though it is the first exposure most readers will have to the marketing problems and opportunities. In a world that travels as fast as does that of marketing, the less knowledge you take for granted, the better off you and your company will be. Don't be verbose but, in a clear manner, try to provide a complete briefing.

THE COMPETITIVE SITUATION.   Markets are, of course, competitive. You should know your competition and gather as much intelligence and data about their activities and achievements as possible. In order to get your market share, you will have to carve out a special niche for your product or service. There is no way in which you can be certain of individuality unless you are aware of what strategic market slots are occupied, by whom, and by what means.

I suggest that at the very least, you should be acutely aware of those major competitors who, in the aggregate, share at least 50–65 percent of any single category of business. You should know the composition of the products and services they offer. You should be aware of their pricing and evaluate it in relation to what your product's pricing is and what your product has to offer. You should know what channels of distribution it is sold through. Are there middlemen involved and how important is the competition's product to the broker or representative who may be selling it? You should have accurate data on the scope of distribution: Is it a nationally or regionally distributed product? Does it have sectional strengths and weaknesses? You should know the financial resources of your competitors. Will they, for example, be able to withstand extra-heavy advertising expenditures on your part to dislodge them from the number-one position? Do they, in other words, have the resources to fight back? If you know the facts, you may be able to put them on the defensive. Are you aware of their advertising strategy? How many dollars do they spend? In what media? Over what period of time and where? With the help of your advertising agency research department you can find this out.

What I am suggesting is that you see yourself in the role of Indian scout or intelligence officer, if you will. In the marketing world, to know the competition is to get the first leg up on beating them to the punch. Many sophisticated marketers will be candid in telling you that the key to their success was not necessarily that they have been smarter or more creative in solving problems. Their secret has been in assembling an apparatus for getting significant amounts of data about their business up on the table. As one chief executive officer put it to me, "If a company has the resources to put itself in the position of knowing as much about a problem as we are able to find out, it's simply a matter of time till we're able to find a marketing edge."

Basically that edge consists of market research. Before proceeding into a more detailed look at the various strategies that make up the total marketing plan, let's look at a few of the questions to which you might want answers.

1. Do you know who your customers are?
2. Do you know where they are located?
3. Have you an understanding of their needs, problems, and wants?
4. Is there any special benefit you offer that the competition doesn't?
5. Where do you want to be in three, five, and ten years? Where are you now?
6. Do your present plans take into consideration all the obstacles and problems you will face?
7. How strong is your intelligence on all aspects of your competition?

The answers to these and other questions will lead you into the development of specific, realistic marketing objectives. These objectives must also be flexible, amenable to each other, measurable, and result-oriented. They should carry an atmosphere of challenge and be considered agreeable by all concerned.

GENERAL ECONOMIC OUTLOOK

No company, brand, service, or business exists in a vacuum. Each is affected by the general prevailing economic climate of the day. Marketers are encouraged to be up on what's going on in the world of business. If inflation runs rampant and tight money policies are the rule of the day, you can and should know that these factors will have an effect on your business. If, for example, imports are being subsidized by the government of exporting countries to the point where your ability to compete with inexpensive labor hinders your competitive pricing, then before you can do something about it, you'll have to be aware of the intricacies and politics of the situation. What, for instance, will be or is our government's prevailing tariff policy? Do you know? High tariffs will protect you—that you should know. What does your industry's trade organization have to say about this? Incidentally, do you know its name or what literature, material, and counsel is available to you? If the cost of financing new plant and equipment appears to be unusually high, are you aware of this? If this is the situation, what implications will it have for your expansion plans? Are the tax rules being changed? Will the changes be favorable to business? Will depreciation legislation make it more or less desirable to speed up your capital expenditures? Each of these few examples may seem like subjects fit only for the deliberations of company presidents and financial vice-presidents. They are not! These factors are no one's exclusive domain. All of these factors and others like them are important for you to be aware of. In the trickle-down nature of the marketing world, they will have an impact on the smaller sphere of the business you will be working on.

Now to some strategic thinking.

STRATEGY SESSIONS

Planning meetings or sessions should cover marketing strategy, which consists of the following areas: product/service strategy, distribution strategy, pricing strategy, sales promotion strategy, and advertising strategy. As you will rapidly see, what I will be covering in this section is the whole as composed of the sum of its various parts. It should essentially indicate to the reader the manner in which the five factors of the marketing mix interrelate for the purpose of being complimentary to and supportive of the broadest business view which is the marketing strategy itself. This, I remind you, is the manner in which resources are planned and their commitment directed so as to achieve specific goals.

Product/Service Strategy

In planning your product or service strategy, you would do well to go back to the genesis of the product for your inspiration. Products do not generally come into being capriciously; there is usually some rhyme or reason for a product or service existing in the first place. As I've indicated to you many times, today's marketer has researched the prospective customer to determine what the needs of the market are. So as a first step, go back to the drawing board and find out what the original intention of the product was. This will shed light on many factors, among them the special attributes of the product which are not necessarily available in its competitors. Starting from this point, you can begin to think strategically.

Please remember, this is the process of determining what you plan to achieve on a long-term basis. For example, will your evaluation of the market situation lead you to the conclusion that you will be satisfied to build a number-two product or service in your category? Or will your thinking be influenced by the noncompetitive nature of the business area you will be going into? If you have something that is unique, how much are you willing to invest to assure that others are discouraged from entertaining the idea of coming into the market? There are many strategic avenues you can explore in your thinking. Each will develop as a result of your analysis of your own specific product or service needs, as reflected by the nature of the market in which it operates.

Today there is much discussion and utilization of one area of strategic market planning which has come to be known as *positioning*. A discussion of its merits will bring you up to date on the most relevant new development in marketing strategy in a good many years. Positioning is a process of thinking about marketing strategy which has as its basis the concept that everything that is made available for sale has a certain degree of competition inherent in the sales situation. This competition can come either from direct competitors or, in the case of one-of-a-kind products or services, from the manner in which consuming groups or institutions choose to spend their disposable incomes. By this I mean that because a product offers something never before available does not mean that it will necessarily be purchased. As appealing as it is, the consuming sector of the market may choose to avoid it completely or may choose to save its money or spend it in another area entirely.

Positioning, in my opinion, is a valuable tool in marketing strategy essentially because it forces the planner to think more realistically about real opportunity areas. It places the ultimate fate of marketing efforts in the hands of the consuming sections of the marketing mix. It acknowledges that not everything can be sold. That is an important point for you to think about. There must be a market for it which is alive and capable of action.

The positioning theory of market planning has many other ramifications. It develops, further, into a full set of tactics for executing the realistic conclusions of its planning stages. But for now, if you are aware that you should consider positioning as an option in developing your strategic thinking, then I will have done my job.

Distribution Strategy

I have found that one of the keys for developing this part of your marketing strategy is an in-depth knowledge of your market. In this section you will want to make some judgment as to how distribution-intensive your product is. By that I mean how important is it to have the product in stores prior to your considering any additional market activity? This might seem to be a rhetorical question, for how can you be expected to sell something that is not available? Let me explain. I am referring herein to the depth of your distribution in stores. Of course the product must be available. But depending upon how you intend to sell your product to the ultimate consumer, you will need lesser or greater amounts of stock at retail. If yours is a product or service that depends on advertising and sales promotion to do the selling for you, you can reduce your efforts in the distribution areas. Consumer demand will force distribution, and you will need more order takers than salesmen. If, on the other hand, what you are marketing cannot be expected to sell through without a product-to-consumer contact being made in a retail environment, then you should develop your distribution strategy around the concept of making certain that it is stocked in depth. In this latter case, the deployment of your financial and personnel resources may well benefit from planning devoted to the establishment of a large and highly efficient sales staff. In preparing this strategy section, you must be wise enough to be aware of the needs to tilt your thinking in several directions, dependent upon what the market situation confronts you with.

Pricing Strategy

The development of an effective pricing strategy will be a result of a variety of factors. The most important of these are the basic economics of your own business—what return will you want on the dollars you have invested to bring a product or service to market? In the business world, financial resources are viewed as assets, and certain yields are expected and required of them.

Pricing is also affected by the efficiency with which you run your business, that is, the cost of bringing a product or service to market. Naturally, if your costs are higher than they should be, you may be tempted to pass them along in the price of your marketed item. Pricing is also determined by the competition and its pricing, as well as the historical pricing record of the item being marketed. Obviously, a simple lead pencil is thought of as a low-priced item. If you are to market one, you must recognize the nature of the price category into which your item fits. Consumers are conditioned over long periods of time to expect to pay a low price for certain items and higher prices for others. Any radical departure will most usually find you pricing yourself out of the market. The consuming groups will find substitute ways of doing the job, and you can be sure that the competition will be watching your actions for any opportunity to take over.

In establishing pricing, the best rule to follow is to always keep the price-value relationship in mind. The best reputation you can build for your product or service is the value image. On a long-term basis, it is the cheapest promotional weapon you will have going for you in your marketing mix. The current trend in the marketplace for higher-priced imported products and services, particularly in certain luxury areas, is the best example I can think of to illustrate the value concept. With the decline of quality in some areas of American goods and services, the consumer has demonstrated her willingness to purchase fewer units if they are better. And quality means better. The consumer is obviously saying she is willing to pay the price if she gets something in return.

Sales Promotion Strategy

To develop this section of your strategy, you must ask yourself a primary question: Does your marketing strategy call for extra inputs of promotional effort to keep it in high velocity? If your answer is yes, then the tools available to you through the sales promotion area should be incorporated as part of your basic strategy. Try to think of sales promotion as an extra bonus effort. If you are like me, you will recognize that it is necessary at prescribed intervals to get marketing momentum going.

Advertising Strategy

Your creative approach, your media approach, and the mood or tone in which advertising is executed are the main ingredients you should consider in the development of your advertising strategy. But before you do any of this, your first step is to reexamine the market situation and establish the importance of advertising in the general mix of marketing activities. Generally, advertising strategies will follow several prescribed patterns. They can be minimal, with the net intent that of doing whatever little is necessary to keep the image alive. Advertising strategy can be primary, also, in that it will be demanded of what you market because you have something important to communicate. Long-range planning demands that you will have to make critical judgments of how much emphasis is to be placed on advertising. Then you will have to live with these judgments. If, for example, your market niche is a low-priced item that offers significant value to the consumer, then you will want to devote as little as possible to advertising. Advertising is a costly venture. You will have to save advertising dollars in order to keep your pricing low. Again, if you have all the data you should have available to you on the composition of the market you will be competing in, then the decisions involved in developing an effective advertising strategy will be revised more easily. I hope that by now you have a more clear-cut feeling for the planning stage of development.

WRITE, WRITE, WRITE!

The time has come to put thoughts to paper and actually write the plan. Knowing where you are going and what you seek to accomplish is dependent on those methods available to you for real action. This section reviews specific plans, including quantitative data you need to complete your written plan and to execute and fulfill the verbal commitment made by all in your strategic planning. It is far too easy to forget the verbal details discussed. The written plan acts as your marketing guide and timetable, as well as a memory jogger for all concerned.

Forecasting Profit and Loss

It is wise to make a hypothetical plan for sales and profit forecasting. This should cover a minimum of ten years' activity. In this section, enlist the aid of your financial people; apply sales and costs estimates to your business. What you will be doing is budgeting and allocating funds for all the various activities in the marketing mix and subtracting the total of these dollars from your anticipated sales forecast. What is left, of course, will be your profit or loss.

Advertising Plan

Develop this on the basis of actual costs of media and production. Include the cost of research. Work with your advertising agency if that is your system, and make certain that they are totally familiar with your marketing plans.

Pricing

Include all the supporting data you can secure on the price composition of your market competitors. It is wise to do a cost per item or unit comparison between your product and the competition. Try to determine if relationships exist between price and marketing success.

Product Service

If you are planning to come to market with something new, you should include a comprehensive assessment of the methods of manufacture, component parts analysis, delivery schedules of components, research and development efforts, and the like. This section should spell out how you can effectively and realistically achieve manufacture of the product or service that has been or is being conceived. The section should provide readers with an overview of the technical side of whatever you plan to market.

Sales Promotion

Draw up a specific plan. It is best to work on a calendar-of-events basis when dealing with the sales promotion specifics of your marketing plan. Demonstrate the timeliness of each activity and, of course, spell out specific costs.

Distribution Plan

This tactical section should include a timetable of events and specifics with regard to pricing which will be offered to customers in the channels of distribution. You should also spell out such things as payment terms, delivery estimates, your returns policy, and cooperative advertising programs, if they are to be made available. It is also advisable to include any plan that covers salesman compensation, special incentives for sales personnel, and, of course, a complete budget breakdown for all activities in the distribution area.

Evaluation

This section should spell out specific criteria that you and all concerned departments will be committed to live by in judging the effectiveness of your total marketing effort. Yes, be specific in setting goals and timetables, and then spell out those techniques you will use to measure the results.

Market plans preparation, as I've stated, has a way of getting away from marketers and running off in many different directions. It is such an important skill for the aspiring marketer that this deficiency in system must be overcome if we are to bring our best to the marketing challenge. Don't try to digest this overview at once. I suggest you go back to it from time to time and amend what I have covered with some experiences of your own. You'll certainly have them.

But keep at it and develop these necessary disciplines. The planning technique will in time alter your thinking to correspond with the long-term nature of the business world you will be entering. Although your progress in any career slot may be judged on what you do for the corporation, today that will only be part of the judgment. As the marketing world continues to become more and more sophisticated, I'm certain that some superior will soon be evaluating you in this important capacity of being able to look down the long marketing road.

IV
TOOLS TO HELP YOU SUCCEED

12
Women
as Managers

Twenty years in marketing, as a consultant to business, a corporate employee, and subsequently a business owner, has taught me much about the process of profit and loss, manufacturing, and the entire field of marketing. During this time a major trend has emerged which is fast becoming an overpowering force in the business community. It is called management science. Businesses are no longer run, they are managed. The trend is an inevitable and rational response to the large scale and proportion of endeavor that is so typical of the American business activity.

THE MANAGEMENT PANACEA

The application of scientific principles or quantitative techniques to all aspects of business management has been very much on the upswing in the last decade. Management science, as it is known, has had a strong impact on the field of marketing. Many readers have probably been exposed to formal training in the management sciences. There are certain reservations about the total management approach that I entertain, certain hesitancies, not with respect to the theory of management per se, but with the manner in which it tends to operate when actually working as a factor in the real-life operations of a corporation. Like many things that are relatively new, management is an outgrowth of many arts and sciences: economics, behavioral science, psychology, and sociology. And it will no doubt be a difficult function to properly administer for the benefit of the general good, the public as well as business. Also, like many things that are new, its arrival has been greeted in many circles as a cure-all for whatever ails the business unit. And that is where the rub is. Companies tend to be overenthusiastic in their embrace of the management method of doing business. With such fervor, they run the classic risk of bureaucratization of the business organization. And with the arrival of the bureaucratic mentality, all that is dynamic within the marketing organization will wither.

Since many women will inevitably find themselves cast in the role of manager, my efforts to cover the intricacies of how an effective management orientation works are very definitely in order. I hope they will land on attentive, if somewhat skeptical, ears. Companies are so often overmanaged and underled. This is a critical factor to comprehend. But inasmuch as management can be an additional weapon in the marketer's arsenal, a review is essential.

Management and Corporate Size

The complexities of contemporary economic life, the very factors that delve into the intricate mix referred to as marketing, demand the presence of effective functionaries. The large corporation must by definition be a group effort. The smaller concern relies more on individual than overall team feeling. The corporation, in its efforts to make the business organization as efficient and therefore as profitable as possible, has adopted a management viewpoint for achieving this end. Essentially, the art of managing involves the direction of efforts to achieve a goal. The way in which the goal is achieved, the planning, organizing, and control of assets utilized to reach such a goal, are the direct responsibility of the manager. As such, it will be the manager's effectiveness and skills in bringing about the desired corporate end that is what one really means when defining managing.

On Being Ready

If an employee has the good fortune to have her job performance come to the attention of senior personnel virtually overnight, that employee could find herself transferred from some basically invisible job to the highly visible area of manager. Be aware of the abruptness with which such change can come about. It can be an unsettling affair if you haven't been preparing yourself for growth. One day a higher-echelon executive might confide some previously confidential piece of company information. The employee's understanding of the system of intracorporate communications should, at this juncture, indicate to her that a new world is being opened. The employee's confidence has been acknowledged in a discreet but very specific manner. Such an action may seem like a passing gesture, but it should not be mistaken for that. It is quite possibly a classic company signal that plans are in the making for your corporate ascendency, that perhaps you might be tapped for the coveted manager's role.

It is suggested that those chosen experience several emotions at this time. They feel gratitude for being among the chosen few; humility, for the task at hand places power in human hands, and that can be a tricky thing to handle; and lastly, a good deal of skepticism. Those chosen will need the latter, for the intricacies of spending most of one's work efforts in a highly subjective, difficult-to-measure, lonely, oftentimes thankless endeavor should give cause to think if the move up is worth the effort.

Identifying the Manager

The new manager should also feel lucky and perhaps give a bit of thanks to her forebears. For notwithstanding the fact that the manager's function can be taught to many, it is more than likely the highly subjective quality referred to as leadership will have influenced the management decision to upgrade an employee's career for the trust he or she has invested. What needs to be emphasized at the outset is that although the skills of the managers can be taught to any reasonably intelligent candidate, the truly effective manager will possess that elusive and ephemeral quality called leadership. If one possesses the leader's trait, the managing task will be much easier. With training in the techniques of management science safely tucked beneath the belt, one's view of management will change also.

Managers will quickly come to agree that managing consists of no more than these techniques utilized by the leader to achieve certain goals. Or, put another way, the role of the manager can be viewed as the natural extension of the leader's personality. It is her way of implementing her will, her way of achieving the ends she has chosen for the department, the division, or even the corporation.

It should be stated at the outset that I have been speaking and thinking of those future managers whose personal aspirations have them seek the top spot as their inevitable destination point. But—and this is important for all initiate marketers to understand—the manager's role and the leadership position that demands mastery of the techniques of managing are not limited to those who aspire to the top. There is much room in the modern corporation for the leader-manager at the three primary levels of the corporation's personnel structure: worker, middle management, and senior management. In each area the skills of the manager can be effectively utilized for achieving goals. Titles and the size of the group involved may seem small to be worthy of the management label. Don't look at the cosmetics; rather, look at the substance of the situation. Titles are not everything! What any participant, regardless of level, will be called upon to do in leading to achieve a goal, will have all the elements of the management function involved. So it is wise to be aware that something as seemingly innocuous as the responsibility of having a secretary or clerk assigned to one's jurisdiction carries with it one of the typical symptoms of the manager's role: the superior-subordinate relationship. Tend, therefore, to this seemingly small first step. It will be worth your while.

MANAGEMENT SKILLS

What are the things considered important for women if they are to effectively execute the manager's function? Books have been devoted to the science of management, and there is but this short chapter to make an effective contribution. Since, however, there are obvious overriding things that affect the manager's role, a discussion of them will be helpful not only in understanding managing but also in preparing for these tasks as future managers of the marketing function.

The qualities that distinguish the manager's role from that of the nonmanager are quite specific. They are the knowledge of the tools of management, the skills of the manager, and the attitude of the manager.

Tools of Management

The effective manager will have human tools, too. She must know, understand, and like to deal with people; she must have a thorough understanding of motivational psychology. Even the assembly line supervisor who has machines to do most of her work must be alert to the facts of life that call for the relief of worker monotony by scheduled break periods. She must also recognize those problems of boredom, which loom menacingly in a highly repetitive and unchallenging job. The alert manager must keep a vigil for the human signs that one day can transform the normally efficient worker into the role of on-the-job trainee. If the manager uses common sense, the task will not be too difficult. And finally, the effective manager will have at her command a strong administrative awareness. She must be able to recognize that in any function to be managed, there will be resources to be gathered and held ready; allocations of time, manpower, machines, and material to be made; and an efficient utilization of these ingredients guaranteed. With these three sets of tools at one's command, the next obvious step is to acquire a set of skills whose utilization will have a direct bearing on how effectively the tools of the manager will be used.

The Skills
of the Manager

The manager must learn how to read the situation. Antennae must constantly be on the alert to the changing environment of the very dynamic, very human business organization. Find out what is really at the heart of the matter; only then will the ability to ponder possible solutions come within one's reach. The second area of skill the manager has to learn lies in the art of decision making. Too often he who hesitates can end up playing catch-up with the competition. The best manager will recognize that it is desirable where appropriate to depersonalize this process. Sometimes doing so can be a tricky thing, for not only will the manager be putting herself on the line, but other personnel will necessarily be exposed.

It is advised to quickly learn the art of decision making. It is the energy element in the management process, and the one too often lacking at all levels of management. Its shortage leads to buck passing. Once the manager has mastered this skill, it is a short move to the third and final skill that is required of all managers. Simply stated, the manager will have to do something. Some action must be executed to put into motion all those resources that will have been gathered to solve any single set of problems. Don't be misguided by the simplicity of this guideline. The entire process of managing is a difficult one because it requires independent activity; this is lonely work. It is so designed by the burdens of what is called the responsibility factor, which is placed on the manager. It is a no-place-to-hide job situation. It is a vulnerable position. It is far easier to put one's finger on the mistakes of the manager than it is to praise a performance well done. Like fine painting, good music, or well-written prose, the good manager's performance will be distinguished by the inability to put one's finger on all the different elements involved in this technique. When working properly, it is the message that comes through that counts. That is the manager's art.

The Attitude
of the Manager

With an understanding of the manager's tools and the manager's skills in hand, we move on now to another area that one should be aware of if a marketing manager's career is to be effective. This is the all-important area of attitude. Your own perspective or points of view as they condition attitudes in the work world will be vital to effectiveness as a manager.

The manager's job is an active, out-front, leading role. It requires an attitude that can get things started. If you are not able to get the ball rolling, to take the first step, then beware the manager's mantle. If your personality bent is such that you would rather be doing than making the doing possible by the environment which the manager must create, then the manager's role is to be avoided.

An increasingly sophisticated and well-informed society is what the manager will be dealing with. This means a better-informed work force, a larger group of educated workers. It will require a shift in focus to the human-relations aspect of the marketing world. The mastery of this art of handling people involved in their relationships within and to the work unit is the primary challenge the manager will face. The art of managing is no less and no more than the art of human relations, with a profit goal as its end objective. And it is a challenging task with many facets, many styles, and many different approaches. Different strategies of management will work, ranging from the autocratic to the freewheeling, even the permissive. The choice is often dictated by the work situation itself. Whatever the manner chosen, people and their interrelationships will always lie at the heart of this problem. This demands that the manager be honest with herself. The manager must be candid in evaluating her own strength and weaknesses. All persons have them. Yes, the manager must look inward before she presumes to make judgments and leadership decisions for others.

In Chapter 1, I pointed out that there are certain aspects of the marketing world that find women in a catch-up or disadvantageous position just because they are women. Prior conditioning has had its effects and women have indeed been prisoners of the fear of success, fear of loss of femininity, and risk-avoiding syndromes. However, it is important to emphasize that at worst, these limitations are transient disadvantages. To a large extent they have been and are being overcome. What has not been emphasized is a plan that women can follow to maximize those positive aspects of the management function that will come as easily to women as to their male counterparts. Incorporate them into your everyday manager's attitude and careers will be enhanced. For simplification, they have been categorized under broad headings.

THE POTENCY OF ATTITUDE AND COMMITMENT.   It's best to look at the marketing world as a positive opportunity. Think positively about everything that is to be done. This is not a Pollyanna approach, and you are not being asked to deny the realities and difficulties that will no doubt arise. But aspiring marketers will find the business world has a funny way of working in their favor if there is the courage to make a commitment to one's convictions. Keep the faith, for in the marketing world, hope springs eternal—and positive thinking is often a self-fulfilling prophecy.

LEARN THE FINE ART OF MANAGEMENT BY GOAL.   Setting goals is not an easy matter, but is an important one. The setting of goals to be achieved is the first step in defining the direction you will lead in your professional and personal life. Goal setting is a way to monitor your progress—or regression. What you want to earn, the job responsibilities you desire, the image you wish to project, the market share your product should obtain—all are goals; all aid you in seeing the light at the end of the tunnel rather than running endlessly in circles.

In this great land of ours, where each and every one of us is trained from childhood to believe that becoming a millionaire or achieving high political office is a realistic possibility, those skills required for the setting of achievable goals are not as easy to master as the aspiring marketer might think. Nonetheless, goal setting has its benefits. From a practical point of view, goals clearly define those all-important aspirational destination points. They also tend to actually simplify the manager's marketing process for, as part of the process of arriving at goals, the manager will have to make distinctions between what is important and what is not. Goal setting is a discipline that can force the manager to think about priorities. Working against predetermined goals eliminates wasted effort and helps the group to cooperate on commonly agreed-upon directions.

Don't set unreasonable goals. Generally speaking, it is always useful to set one's sights just a little bit higher than what you may reasonably expect to achieve. Not unconscionably high, for this is a futile exercise. Keep goals up there, for it is never too late to come down a bit. A price reduction is always in order, but obviously, getting the full retail price is preferable.

RECHARGE YOUR NEGATIVE/POSITIVE BATTERY.   The potent marketing manager will be alert to the opportunities that often lurk in the shadow of defeat. This is an attitude and skill that is smart to learn. The business world is each and every day treated to the lesson of the comeback or the turnaround situation. The apparent mystery of why companies seem to go through wave after wave of marketing changes is not so mysterious when closely examined. It is because of their firm belief that grasping victory from the jaws of defeat can best be executed and is dependent upon a certain species of managerial wisdom. There is that person who does her best when things are at their lowest ebb. This is a pressure worker. This positive thinker is a unique breed. Characteristically, she will have vision and flexibility. Often her actions are seemingly simple. It is her ability to look in other directions for solutions—her unstructured approach—that is her most valuable asset.

MASTER THE ART OF CONFLICT RESOLUTION.   One of the most useful skills the manager can employ will be the ability to make subordinates utilize their tensions in a constructive manner. Tension is misunderstood. It is not all bad. A certain amount of it can be motivating and is indeed required if the manager is not to have a group of limp dolls on her hands. It is a misdirected tension, one that grows into hostility and then gives birth to conflict between persons, that is what the manager will have to be mindful of.

There is a growing area known as business psychiatry. The emphasis in the corporate world insofar as the human resources activity is concerned has been to find techniques that unleash hidden creative talents. Such things as self-actualization, consciousness raising, and the like have been tried with varying degrees of success and failure.

If there is, in fact, a psychiatric bottom line, then one would be well advised to pay close attention to this new phenomenon. The business psychiatrist has achieved startling results in the area of executive and worker productivity by applying techniques learned in family therapy practice to the corporate world. Think of those who have to be managed as you would manage the members of a family unit, with all the sibling rivalries, feud-making tensions, differing points of view, and superior, subordinate, and peer group relationships. The next thought will be a logical one: Women are eminently better qualified than are men to practice those techniques of cooperation, accommodation, mutual sharing, motivation, commitment, and loyalty that are the bedrock upon which family unity is built. Women are better qualified than their male colleagues whose energies have most probably been directed in less-human-directed pursuits. Men are just now beginning to learn some of the real burdens associated with the personal and intimate areas of family life. So, women do indeed have the competitive edge. Women are used to utilizing those bits and pieces of female wisdom that are their birthright. These are some of the most practical tools available for the resolution of intracorporate conflict.

View the marketing group, however large or small, as persons transferred for a prescribed number of hours each day into a corporate family. The goal, of course, is to resolve conflict situations and make seemingly conflicting, even irreconcilable points of view bend just enough to accomplish the common-good task at hand. The business psychiatrist has been and is doing this. The smart manager can do equally well.

No discussion of the art of management would be complete if it did not cover the last major point I wish to make in this chapter. As I previously noted, there is an aura around the management science about which I have some hesitancies. It is the rush to accept it as the new gospel that is disturbing. I have attempted to demonstrate that the gospel—management religion, if you will—comes a little easier if some mature and practical perspective is applied. There are few, if any, strict orthodoxies when it comes to the world of marketing, and the management function is really no exception. What leads me again to this conclusion is an analysis of the fine art of verbal communication in the manager's world. It can be seen as an attempt to mystify the manager's role, thus raising it in the corporate hierarchy. As it has developed, this language is now in place. It is used. So, for better or worse, in an attempt to lighten the seriousness that has been brought to the entire subject, it should be dealt with. It comes with the manager's territory.

LINGO OF MANAGEMENT

The lingo of management is highly imaginative and is designed, characteristically, to enable you to make a point in shorthand. Perhaps it is an outgrowth of the need to save time when communicating in the hectic manager's world. In any event, it is graphic and can be effective. Learn the language so the terms will be easy to understand. A complete dictionary is of course impossible. But to provide some insight, certain prime areas can be covered. The following short glossary of terms is based on commonly accepted usage. Much like a guidebook for traveling in foreign countries, this glossary will help in management country. Until women have lived in it for a short while, the glossary will ease the pain of travel.

Glossary of Management Terms

POLICY. This is the net effect of a course of action that has traveled the full route of manager's interests. After carefully weighing all the factors involved in any one area of business activity and viewing alternative courses of action, an agreement has been reached that has the force of finality. Policy usually refers to very important matters. A distinction should be made between a policy and a decision. Policy is usually effective for a long period of time, whereas decisions are actions taken on matters that govern shorter periods of activity. A series of decisions may and oftentimes do lead to the making of a policy.

TIME FRAME. This means the actual time limitations expressed in hours, days, weeks, or months, within which some action must be completed. Time frames are usually established by looking toward the last possible completion date of any one activity. From this point, one figures backward to the present. Managers utilize a time frame to schedule and plan. Many marketing managers plan their activities on a customer time frame basis. That is, they plan activities from that date at which the end user of the product or service involved can normally be expected to take consuming action.

PLAY BACK. The fast pace of the manager's everyday work world requires a good deal of verbal transmission. Often, such communication takes place while the worker is engaged in some other activity. To ensure that one has received the message that has been transmitted, the practice has developed of repeating instructions to the sender. Playing it back means "This is how I understand what you have just said." In the playback mechanism, adjustments and sometimes additions are made. These can be affirmed and acknowledged by a second playback. The point of the playback is understanding and comprehension.

HIP SHOOTING. This is a reference to the style and personality of another. It is meant to categorize the actions or words of another person as being precipitous and not well thought through. Hip shooting is frowned upon. It is perceived as the action of a person who will give any answer simply for the sake of appearing responsive. It's desirable to avoid it. Better to ask for additional time and come back at a later date with a well-thought-through response. Hip shooters have, unfortunately, developed their skills to a high degree. Their answers oftentimes convey the image of substance and in this regard can be dangerous.

STROKING.   There is a fine but significant line of difference between the manager who will stroke an employee or superior and the manager who polishes an apple. Stroking is the legitimate application of charm to achieve an end. Apple polishers are solely dependent on flattery to make a point or gain advantage. The easiest way to determine the difference is to watch the frequency with which each of these techniques is used. Stroking is usually engaged in sparingly. It is called upon in special situations. The apple polisher, on the other hand, will most likely depend on this technique as a principal method of persuasion and communication. It is seldom effective.

NO WIN.   There will be circumstances in the life of the manager when there is no possibility of achieving a desirable end. Managers are sometimes caught in these no-win situations. When confronted with a situation like this, it is best to minimize losses and accept the setback gracefully.

MODELING.   This refers to the process used for testing purposes in which a representative and, by definition, smaller-than-the-whole sample of something is constructed. The purpose of modeling is to limit the cost involved in making a marketing decision. Modeling is also used to predict actions and activity. It is the same process used in forecasting election results by projecting from a small group of key and demographically representative percentages those actions of all demographically matching precincts in the universe being studied.

UPWARD MOBILITY.   This is a personnel term used to describe the attitude of a person whose aspirations are for a better life. It is used to characterize the person or persons within the group who have been identified by their peers as being on the way to success. It is an aspirational term.

OPEN END.   This is the manager's way of saying she has decided to leave the decision-making time a thing of the future. It implies that other data will be needed and is probably forthcoming. It is meant to refer to those things that are believed to be resolvable, but for which the final keys to resolution are not yet available.

COMMUNICATIONS PROBLEM.   This is a bureaucratically induced euphemism for not taking some action because some participant dropped the ball.

QUANTIFY.   This term derives from the research field. It means that whatever may have just been said has the ring of truth, but will only be acceptable if a large number of people or their actions can be introduced as proof that makes the same point. Though 50 million Frenchmen can indeed be wrong, the comfort given by a large number of persons attesting to the same activity carries considerable weight in arguing a point.

ROLE REVERSAL.   This refers to a technique used by managers which asks any two persons involved in discussing a business point of view to consciously assume the role of the other. For example, if you are intent on selling a certain point of view, the person to whom you are trying to make the sale will assume your role; conversely, you will assume hers. Role playing is a device used to test theories and to gain perspective by forcing persons to see the other point of view. It is quite useful in training the manager for higher levels of executive responsibility.

GO/NO GO.   This refers to the process of taking a matter to a certain prescribed point, at which time a decision for or against it will be made. The value in the go/no go method is that no prior commitment is implied; thus, participants in the process are encouraged to be as forthright in their recommendations as possible.

Managing the marketing function is a skill to be learned along with all the other skills and talents women in marketing will need. Women should be aware that such techniques exist. Utilization of certain techniques will provide solutions to otherwise unsolvable personnel dilemmas. Precipitous firings and hirings can be damaging to the efforts and spirit of the marketing organization. Utilizing certain management techniques—those that especially suit one's own personal style—can go a long way toward making the marketing day a shorter and more fruitful one.

13

Survival Techniques: You'll Need Them

The nature of survival in the corporate world is such a personal undertaking that I hope to underscore the impact that an incorporation of these techniques can and should have on the marketer.

Experience has taught me that the old byword "Live to fight another day" is very much applicable to what women can expect to find as they enter the world of marketing—helpful hints for surviving in corporate America. I guess these, as much as anything else, can be credited for getting me to the point of being able to share some words of wisdom with you. One of the keys to mastering these survival tactics is to review them periodically and to adapt them to your particular circumstances.

My list of survival techniques may have some variances with respect to gender, but for the most part I don't view them as behavior patterns that have come about as a result of the major role women now play as marketers. Instead, they reflect what I have time and time again said—that is, that man is a political animal. My suggestion is not necessarily that you become a politician, for that person's end goals are all too often power, and the corporation be damned. What I do believe, though, is that you owe it to yourself to assemble a set of techniques that will support your competitive and assertive activities. Using these, and viewing them in a positive sense, you will then be able to make a contribution to the corporation. These techniques have earned their battle scars. They allow you the forum—within the corporation—to air your views. Thus, given the opportunity for a day in court, should you not prevail, it will more than likely be for some substantive fundamental marketing error you have made. At least you will have been playing the game under the rules of the gentlewoman.

With this advice in mind, I'd like to have you proceed with me through a little play. The setting is your first major marketing plans meeting. All the characters will be in attendance: the marketing director, various brand managers, perhaps your division president, and some representatives of your advertising and promotion agencies. As is the way in the marketing world, this happening is about to take place in Conference Room A. It will most likely be a Spartan-looking room. There will be a conference table, pads and pencils neatly assembled, and perhaps some audiovisual equipment, and, of course, a blackboard. Not exactly a cheery or comforting environment, but fields of play never are, unless you are a spectator.

At this very moment the first of my set of survival techniques should start operating. They have to do, in the main, with how you approach the meeting. Let's call them meeting manners. Here goes. Never be the first or the last to arrive—it gives you away as too eager or, worse, not caring. Next, where to sit? I advise near the head man or woman, if at all possible. This will at once give you an air of confidence, for only the fainthearted sneak to the back of the room. Once everyone has been seated, a good move is to be the first to put that impressive-looking portfolio of papers on the table. Now, look around you. Is the entire room in shirt-sleeves? If so, let that be your cue to keep your jacket on, or vice versa. Going against the odds in this situation positions you as a dedicated professional. The first time I witnessed this action, I was convinced that this person was both ready to work and, more importantly, better prepared for whatever might come. Now's the time to sit back from the table—just a bit farther back than the others. It will give you a chance to view the entire scene for peer reaction without being obvious. Remember, this is a dynamic, interrelating group of personalities you will be sitting with. Best to give yourself a chance to size them up.

Once the meeting has been called to order, it's wise to take notes. I suggest you jot down the date, names of participants, and subject matter of the meeting. This is always a good starting point, and will help you keep track of the meeting's proceedings as they develop. One final note as to deportment. If there is water on the table, be certain not to drink too much. If you're nervous, and this is normal in such situations, the pouring action (a trembling hand) might give you away. And what's more, there will always be some cynical soul in the group who may think you are compensating for having been out too late the previous evening. Now that everyone is settled in, the action is about to begin.

The second phase of survival tactics comes under the broad

category I refer to as executing the presentation. Firstly, always try to avoid being the first presenter. In so doing, you get a chance to size up the general atmosphere in the room. If one or more of your colleagues presents ideas similar to yours and they meet with disapproval, it gives you the chance to scratch that idea before you present yours. Likewise, if an idea similar to yours meets with approval, use it to your advantage by reminding the group they liked it before by saying something like, "I agree with Jim's thinking that . . ." and so on. Thus you have shared the credit for the idea and reinforced its merits as well. Jim might not be too thrilled with you, but that's part of the business game plan played in countless corporations daily.

Assuming you could not get moved along on the list and you are the first presenter, never, never present your best idea first. Let's assume you have been asked to present your view on the selection of test markets for a new product. Since this area of marketing is traditionally marked by varying schools of thought, you can rest assured that whatever your point of view, you will have many detractors and many benefactors. Assuming there are several options presented about which the group will express its opinion, by saying your real preference for last you will have deflated the high energy level of the assembled group, which for some reason or another will strike down the first few ideas presented to them as though this were a mandatory action. Since the creative process focuses on a marketing solution, your first and most instinctive ideas will be your best. It is folly not to protect them from the overanxious group. Let your first presentations act as scouts, assessing the strength and preferences of the assembled group. Only after you have gotten back this initial intelligence can you safely proceed with what you really feel is first-rate.

Once you have gotten to the point of being able to present what you think is the best solution to the problem, the manner and tone in which you speak and act will be significant. Avoid overenthusiasm, yet maintain an air of confidence. A confident manner goes much further than the overkill that is the by-product of overenthusiasm. In a word, try to be firm and yet low-key. Even modesty is preferable to the bluster of hard sell, for modesty tends to disarm people and make them comfortable, and only then will they really be hearing what you have to say.

Another tip you should follow religiously is to concentrate the substance of your remarks on the big picture. Have a flow and logic to your presentation, but try to make it look simple and carefree. Otherwise your message will be that of the person who is trying too hard. Try to keep the amount of detail you must include to a minimum. Believe me when I say that many a great concept has been thrown into the trash can because some detractor or critic in the room has seized upon a minor point in the presentation and found error with it. Be smart; don't relegate the larger concept to the area of the might-have-been.

A third and major strategy for surviving the meeting is what I refer to as the "get smart, get with it" system. What I have found is that a good listener can assess the tone and flow of the meeting and turn this mood to his or her advantage. Each and every meeting you attend will be different, because people are different. The days of the week differ, the weather is different, and so on. What I am saying here is that one has to develop the facility I call listening along. Obviously, some days will be easier for you than others, but assuming that in the main these meetings will be tough and competitive, then your ability to read the mood of the assembled group is going to be critical to success.

Some advice on the matter of criticism. Listen well, for the manner in which you accept it will condition your own methods for giving it. It is wise never to be overly critical of another's work. Tact and diplomacy on your part in the meeting room may well earn you the same gesture in return. And be prepared for criticism from even your best friends. All loyalties have a way of falling to the wayside when the general consensus in the room is against you. If the road to ruin is paved with good intentions, beware the well-intentioned friend.

Continuing with our hypothetical meeting, it's now about 3:15. Three of your colleagues have had a turn at bat, and you're sure to be next. You've surely learned something sitting there taking notes for over an hour. I suggest you make it all work for you as follows: Tailor your presentation to eliminate any obvious mistakes that have surfaced in the presentations of others. For example, if the favorite marketing word of the week, "share of mind," is not being well received that day, think about using the phrase "What degree of the consumer's consciousness can we expect to penetrate?" Benefit from the mistakes of your peers by focusing the thrust of your efforts against a strategy that seeks to place the competition in the position of the enemy. Rise above the competitive style of your peers, regardless of how forceful their remarks may have been. Remember, you're not in that meeting to win awards from your peers, but rather to do in the competition. And try to link your efforts, no matter how superior to the group's they may be, to a philosophic mood and tone that spell out the key word, *cooperation*. Praise those who have preceded you and try, if possible, to demonstrate how your point of view complements and dovetails with those that have already been presented.

The clock moves forward toward the end of the meeting. The last set of survival rules are every bit as important as the previous ones. I know, because I have experienced it many times, that by now your own energy level will have diminished to the point of no return. If first impressions in meetings are important, then last or exit impressions are every bit as important to your survival.

Here are my tips: I call this area strategic exiting. Don't leave anything behind. Carelessly strewn notes leave an impression that you are a one-shot person. Collect your notes; be as organized when you leave as you were when you entered. What's more, there's vital intelligence in your jottings, and in a competitive environment, you may want to think twice before leaving your hard-earned knowledge out there for easy removal. When you do leave the meeting, be gracious; if possible, chat a while with those in attendance. You may catch a hint as to the post mortems, which will prepare you better for the next gathering. In addition, sticking around eliminates you as a target for the post mortems. And finally, allow yourself a smile, but don't be too cheerful, even if you have won the day. In the world of marketing, it's bad form. Save the celebration for later that evening—and by all means, have yourself a great one!

So far, this chapter has dealt with techniques for survival that center around the group meeting. I think you will already agree with me that their presentation as part of this book tells you how strongly I feel about their utilization. You may be shocked or taken aback at the somewhat realistic approach these techniques take. If so, I can only say to you that they are the product of many victories and many defeats in the marketing arena. I hope they will help you, and I sincerely think they will.

MEMORANDUM WRITING: A VERY VALUABLE SKILL

There is a second broad area I believe is important to include in this survival tactic section. It is the area that concentrates on the nonverbal side of the marketer's role in the organization. I refer to the fine art of written communication and its dissemination, as found in the all-too-famous memorandum. How to prepare it, what to do and what not to do with it are all part of the game. Like it or not, sometimes you'll be forced to be an active player. Now for some do's and don'ts.

There is real power in a memorandum. The mere fact that someone has taken the time and effort to commit something on paper will suggest to the recipient that what is contained in the memorandum is important. A picture may well be worth a thousand words, but in corporate America, "first came the word" is as true today as ever. The basic utility of the form of communication known as the memo is to inform someone of some action. Unlike a verbal transaction, which cannot be recorded or verified, and is often not remembered, the memorandum is considered an official sign, a blessing from on high. Such is the force of words on paper. Of course, not all memorandums are written by those at the top of the corporate ladder. There will be many lateral memos, ascending memos to superiors, and flexible memos whose distribution structure cuts across all levels in the corporation. If you are smart and alert, you will pay heed to those innocent-looking pieces of paper, for their power lies not only in what they say, but in the method in which they are used.

You may think I am placing too much emphasis on the use of the memorandum, but I assure you it is a sign of your competence that people will be watching closely. Mastery of the memo-writing methodology will say much about you. Primarily, the person who properly prepares a memorandum will be demonstrating to the organization much about her knowledge of the corporation's political structure and the rules of etiquette, and, though some would argue the point, will indicate that you have mastered a command of the English language to a sufficient degree to get your message across. I cannot make this last point emphatically enough. As we move headlong into the electronic/video age, the inability to overcome deficiencies in written communications are probably understandable, but in no sense do I find them acceptable.

I hope I have convinced you of the value you should place on the properly prepared memorandum. Now let me give you some helpful hints as to how to prepare and use one. The first item I'd like to address myself to is the logical and obvious question: When is a memorandum in order? I have found that any time a business circumstance arises that requires a next step or follow-through, it is advisable to put it on paper. For example, if you plan to proceed with the development of package designs for a new product, and the meeting you have just attended has discussed this, but the next steps were not clearly spelled out, then the writing of a memorandum will get the subject on the table. All too often it has been my unhappy experience that meetings of large groups disperse, and none of the participants come away with the same impression of what has happened. So put it on paper. If your plans are not what the group feels they had decided, then believe me, you will hear about it.

Another perfect time for memo writing is when a new idea occurs to you and you want to get some reaction to it from your superiors. Spell it out in a memo. The boss, if he is managing his time properly, will probably devote a certain period of his day to reading correspondence from the staff. Your memo will both inform him and let him know, because it is in writing, that it is your idea. I find that it is generally a good idea to place in memorandum form any activity you are involved in within the corporation that can cause an expenditure of corporate funds to take place.

Sometimes you will find the writing of a memorandum useful for refreshing your own memory. On such occasion a memorandum for the file will give you a permanent record of some thought or action you do not want to make public at that time but think may have utility later on. The general rule for memo writing is not to overdo it, but if your own good judgment tells you an idea is worthy of exposure or needs the verification power and the authority that only the memo can provide, then by all means get your pencil and paper out.

Now that you know some general reasons for memorandum preparation and the role that this document plays in corporate life, I'm going to let you in on some seemingly innocent guidelines for the correct preparation and distribution of said memorandum. Follow them closely. First on the list is the matter of memo style. There's a right way and a wrong way to prepare one, and people can get awfully fussy about this. Incidentally, what makes style so important is the need to make the memo an easy thing for the receiver to digest. Yours will be one of a multitude of pieces of paper that may cross a recipient's desk during the course of the day. You will be doing yourself a favor if you ease the comprehension burden for the reader.

The first rule has to do with what is called the pecking order. This is a reflection of the power structure within the organization. What it usually means is that the woman or man at the top of the heap finds her or his name at the top of the memo. All other recipients are then listed in descending order of importance. Some organizations have adopted a more democratic form and, instead, choose to alphabetize. This technique is fine, but you'd be wise to check your organization and find out what older hands than yours are doing. Follow their style. In order to eliminate any confusion about whom the memorandum is intended for and the subject matter to be discussed, be certain to use the *To, From, and Subject* memorandum structure. The reader's attention will immediately be flagged, and he or she will have the luxury of being able to determine just how urgent your memorandum is on the long list of paperwork that must be covered. Following this structure or format is a nice gesture on your part. I find it's not often forgotten.

Now a word about subjects. Be specific. If your subject matter is advertising expenditures, spell out the detail. For example, the wrong way to refer to an advertising topic is to title your memorandum *TV Advertising* when what you really intend to discuss is *Production Cost of a 30-Second Videotape Commercial.*

And finally, in the matter of form, always place a date on your memorandum and make sure that the entire memo is neat and tidy. In any corporation there are always the realities of time and deadlines at work. A memorandum that cannot give the reader a frame of reference with respect to time and isn't neat tends to say that the writer doesn't care about the time pressures of others within the organization. The sloppiness of the final document will add to the impression of limited commitment on the part of the writer.

Another primary purpose of the memorandum is to get some action going. In order to handle this properly, you can help yourself by paying close attention to action devices. If you expect a response, then ask for it. This can take the form of "Please let me know what your thoughts are," or, if the channels of communication so dictate, ask the recipients to "Alert the sales department." In some organizations the lines through which instructions flow are very clearly spelled out. Get to know the proper flow of these communications channels; pay attention to them in your memos. The area of action is a tough one, and sometimes it requires a little prodding. Remember, everyone in the corporation will probably be as busy as you are, so the marketer who takes affront at not having immediate action taken on her proposal can be a source of tension. If you honestly feel that enough time has passed for any reasonable colleague to get back to you, then I believe a reminder memo is in order. As in memo writing in general, never write this kind of memo when you are angry. It's natural and healthy to feel this way sometimes, but losing your cool is one of the no-no's of corporate etiquette. Control your hostility and instead search for some logical reason that will give you a premise for the reminder. Perhaps you will want to pass along additional data which "may be useful to you in formulating a response." Or perhaps something has taken place in the marketplace that will affect the response. Try, at all costs, not to crowd your recipient. The reminder that gets the job done is usually one that makes the nature of the request seem secondary to other purposes for which the memo is written. You and I know that this is not the case, but leaving your recipient a graceful opportunity to save face for being late will do wonders to get that action you so eagerly desire.

There is one additional area of memo writing that I've always found useful. This has to do with those times, and there will be a sufficient number of them, when it will be best to curl up that piece of paper and throw it into the trash basket. Sometimes the best memo is the one that's never sent. I am the first to admit that knowing what to communicate openly for all to see is a delicate matter. As marketers, you will be expected to be wise enough to master these ground rules. They can serve you well. Most of these areas have to do with matters that can affect a person's career. If you have to convey some criticism or evaluations, do it in face-to-face discussions behind closed doors. You may be forced at some later date to commit to writing the circumstances and substance of your critique, but by that time other solutions may have been found. At the very least, you will have proven that your critique is not a personal matter. Never spell out a person's faults in a memo. Never threaten, coerce, or otherwise commit yourself to some severe course of action, such as docking pay or dismissal, unless you are prepared to stand behind your words. If you do find that you are in a position where such a memo is required, then it should be marked confidential. Make sure that only you and the recipient have copies.

And finally, I want to mention the matter of multiple copies. The famous corporate carbon dilemma is a very real one. I have always been successful by following a rule that is an outgrowth of executive administration in the intelligence community. It's called "the need to know." You'll always be on the safe side of discretion if you ask yourself the question, Does he or she really need the information in order to function in the job? If the answer is no, you will have reduced the paperwork-clutter problems and probably spared several bruised egos. Naturally, if all or the majority of persons in the group you are working with are involved in the subject matter your memo covers, then everyone should get a copy. In this case, judgment will tell you when it may be important to bend the "need to know" rule a bit; that extra copy or two will most certainly not overwhelm your secretary.

The last area I think is important for you to include among your list of survival techniques is a specialized one. It has to do with the special situations women find themselves in as they progress in the marketing world. Please be advised, if you do not already know, that although women will find the greatest degree of reward and personal satisfaction in acting as women, the rule of corporate etiquette has long since been set by men. Until such time as the style of how one should conduct oneself changes, and it surely will, I think a word to the wise is sufficient.

I call this area of business etiquette "follow the leader." Watch what she or he does and emulate the same set of manners. Chances are you'll be thought of more as a businessperson and colleague than as a woman.

There are some tactics that will help you fit into the group and prevent your male colleagues from feeling any embarrassment at your presence. The most important general guideline is to make light of things. Don't let minor issues blow up out of proportion, for then you will most assuredly be accused by those venerable gentlemen who have been setting the tone and pace of things of acting "like a woman." If, for instance, the gesture of holding the door for you or helping you with your coat is accomplished with an overdone gesture, then you can readily assume that you have run into a resident male chauvinist. Ignore it the first time and be sure to avoid getting yourself into that position with the same individual again. If it happens again, take a position and let him know that such patronizing acts are recognized for what they are.

But also be sure to tell the group who may witness such behavior that you recognize this fellow is the exception to the rule. On the matter of greeting people, make the first effort and offer your hand to be shaken. Men are somewhat hesitant about this, so you will be helping your new associates out of an uncomfortable spot.

Now, perhaps you find yourself seated in your office busily concentrating on some papers. When a visitor enters, make certain that you do as your mother probably taught you long ago. Just rise to your feet to greet the visitor. Again, plain good sense and the manners you were brought up with will help you.

Phone calls, too, have their own set of rules. If that visitor is still with you and the telephone rings, ask that your calls be held till such time as you can conveniently return them. Talking on the phone while a new arrival sits by patiently is perceived as a rude gesture. If it is so urgent a call that it cannot wait, answer the call with your name rather than a standard hello. If you have to phone the caller back, at least he will know that you have taken the time to identify yourself, and he'll feel more comfortable while he's waiting to hear back from you.

The matter of signatures and business cards is also easily handled. When it comes to gender designations like Mr., Miss, Mrs., or the current Ms., simply omit any designation. Unless you are named after a long line of male ancestors, it is more than likely that your name alone will identify your gender.

What to do when it comes to check-paying time in a restaurant? That's an easy one. With male co-workers, unless it's an expense-account item, simply do as the Dutch do and pay your share. You should do this every time. Men will respect you for this, and once they see that you fully intend to pay your share of the freight, any notions they might have about pegging you as something less than equal will have been dissipated. The point is simple: If you prove your worth in money matters, the work matters will be an easier barrier to hurdle.

If you are taking a client to lunch, things shouldn't be too difficult. When the check arrives, casually put it next to your place without even a pause in the conversation. This gives the clue that you plan to pay. If your client balks, explain that it is standard procedure for you to treat clients. If he still complains, bow gracefully to his demands—this time. Next time, arrange to leave your credit card with the maitre d' so that when the invoice is presented at the table, so is the credit charge—all you have to do then is sign! No fuss, no conversations.

Now, two last points. Again, this may seem to have little to do with what you view as survival tactics. But remember, in the world of the corporation, most people will judge you on what you appear to be, not necessarily on what the inner you really is. So when you're out in a group with other executives, by no means hold a door open for senior executives. Let someone else do that. You may well be in the company of older gentlemen who will take the gesture of door holding as being a sign of brashness on your part. Schooled in older ways, these gentlemen have a curious and complex etiquette code. They will think little of being at the head of the pack when a group of executives must be led down the hall to a meeting room, but they revert to older ways when it comes to allowing a lady to do something so physical as holding the door. If just you and the gentleman are together, let him precede you through the open door and just hope that he will have had the good sense to open it for the two of you.

I hope these techniques for survival will be as helpful to you as they have been in my career. Naturally, there are many circumstances that will arise to test your imagination. There will be many times when you will wish that an obvious solution to a sticky problem would come readily to mind. I can assure you that these times will come—and when you least expect them. But if I have convinced you of the need to at least think about these areas, then I believe the exception to the rule will find you in a better and stronger position to deal with it.

14

The Art of Marketing the Marketing Woman

Recognition that the marketing approach used to move goods and services can also be applied to the transaction known as moving people, otherwise defined as the area of human resource development, is an interesting corollary of the marketing theories developed in this book. For the marketing woman who is either at an entry level or who has reached a more mature career position, a review of the specific tactical approach for implementing her own marketing strategies for advance and/or career change is in order.

Government statistics indicate that no less than 90 percent of all employed persons, both women and men, express less than a complete level of satisfaction with the career positions they currently hold. The statistic is startling in and of itself, and also gives a significant clue as to one of the prerequisites for success in the marketing world. Realistically, the implication is clear that the woman marketer will have to build a base of assets outside her own job accomplishment areas which she can and most probably will have to call upon one day to further her career.

In classic marketing terms, if the woman executive views herself and her capabilities as the product or service to be marketed, she will be charged, first and foremost, with relating her own benefits as a marketable commodity to those market segments that may have specific need for her. Her first task will be to identify these markets. The marketing of human resources is in many respects more difficult than is that of product or service marketing, primarily because the nature of the consuming markets is not so clearly delineated. This market is said to be a hidden one, with many of the characteristics of the treacherous iceberg, whose real power lies hidden, for the most part. Nonetheless, there are certain known characteristics of the dynamics of this market. Essentially, the human resource market seeks product satisfaction on two dimensions: the need to be aware that certain specific talents are available in certain personnel, and the need for an interrelating information transmittal system with its sister markets, which can facilitate the exchange of information about these available human resources. With these two product attributes and an understanding of their dynamics, the astute marketer will be able to develop a set of tactics for satisfying the market needs.

In traditional markets, research would be utilized to cull out those market segments and the benefits they require for satisfaction prior to the undertaking of a specific position for the product. Happily, a wide body of experience already exists with data in support of it that eliminates this segment of the marketing task. The dynamics of the market—talent awareness and information transmittal—has already been established. What remains, and the matters to which the substance of this chapter will be devoted, is the identification of the specific market segments and a review of viable techniques for bridging the market-product gap.

The human resources market can be said to be composed of five parts: the professional association, peer/colleague socializing, civic/community/political involvement, the publishing segment, and the teaching and lecturing segment. Each, as previously mentioned, contains the personality traits of the iceberg in that its stated and intended purpose is in each case only a part of the true function. Each holds as an area of its own benefit/reward the compilation of data on available personnel and a quid pro quo understanding that it will transmit such data to other segments of the human resources market in exchange for similar information. From a marketer's point of view, this market is indeed traditional. It knows what it needs and what will satisfy it, and it is available or reachable from what marketers would consider a distribution point of view. Specifically, it sets up channels of distribution in which goods and services—in this case, personnel—can be viewed, put on display, and merchandised in a manner that will allow for a purchase decision to be made by the consuming group. A review of these five segments of the human resources market is in order.

THE PROFESSIONAL ASSOCIATION

Each month of the year, usually on a specific day of the week, in major marketing centers around the country—New York, Chicago, Dallas, San Francisco, Cleveland, Detroit, Boston, and many others—usually to the accompaniment of some prefatory cocktails and a chicken-and-peas dinner, a host organization will provide a luncheon environment for the presentation of a paper, a case history, a new technique, or a point of view directly related to the conduct of operations and thinking in the world of marketing. Gathered to pay attention to the speaker—a company president, research analyst, marketing manager, advertising agency executive, or marketing consultant—will be those members of the professional membership's organization. These are individuals whose avowed and, indeed, primary purpose for membership in the likes of the Sales Executive Club, The American Management Association, The Society of Security Analysts, or Marketing Communications Executives International will be to gather knowledge and learn new techniques that will assist them and those companies they work for to satisfy more professionally some marketing task. And, true, much will be learned by these attendees. In the process, the aspiring woman marketer will have the opportunity to expose herself as either a speaker or a panel participant; or, if she attends as a nonparticipant, she will be in the enviable position of extending her list of contacts beyond those of her own business organization. The unwritten rules of the game are that a little discreet personal selling and horn blowing are allowed at such association gatherings, provided they don't become too obvious. The aspiring woman marketer will do well to at least make her availability known as one who is willing to undertake some unsung task of the organization, such as publicity development, membership solicitation, telephone task forces, and the hundred and one other seemingly nonrewarding tasks which the association will look to its members to involve themselves in. Such participation will, over the long term, often lead to an invitation to join the board of such professional organizations, and soon the marketer's name may appear on official letters and other communication documents of the association. Such seemingly innocent beginnings will, as they have many times, soon lead to an awareness of the marketer. This is the first step in reaching the hidden human resources market. Someone's credentials and very existence—perhaps yours—have been acknowledged by the group. The human resources market has had the opportunity to identify a new and possibly consumable product.

PEER/COLLEAGUE SOCIALIZING

Over the years there have been many schools of thought with respect to the advisability of mixing one's business and social life. Though some highly conservative corporations frown on the practice, or prescribe certain limitations to it—we're all aware of company picnics, office parties, retirement dinners, and the like—the practice of after-work cocktails, parties, and other peer-and-superior social intermingling is a practical approach to penetrating a human resources market. It is in such informal settings, where the talk is often of some work-connected topic, that the aspiring marketer has the opportunity not only to display her marketing wares to peers and perhaps those higher up on the scale, but also to expose herself to members of other organizations who are often invited to join.

CIVIC/COMMUNITY/POLITICAL INVOLVEMENT

In that arena of the human resources marketplace where the true measure of a woman may be taken with respect to personal attitudes held and the skills of fact and diplomacy utilized in espousing such attitudes as are readily discernible for all to see, the woman marketer will find ample opportunity for a linkage to kindred spirits. These can serve her own career ascendancy goals. A local political action club or participation in a civic drive such as a Red Cross fund raiser, the United Way, and similar undertakings, all can provide the marketer the opportunity to display the marketer's skills in a nonprofit and presumably selfless undertaking. Wise marketers should be aware that those in charge of such undertakings will be consciously assessing the level of marketing skills that the volunteers bring to the community activity. Such assessments are cataloged and stored away for future use by leaders. These leaders are always on the lookout for demonstrations of unusual talent and ability. Given the proper circumstances, they will call upon such personnel to transfer these civic-directed skills to the marketing needs of a business organization.

THE PUBLISHING SEGMENT

Articles preparation, including papers and points of view about current marketing problems rank among the best avenues for creating awareness of oneself as an on-the-move personality in the human resources marketplace. Starting with those trade periodicals that are read on a fairly regular basis, the aspiring marketer will more often than not find that a by-lined article in the likes of *Advertising Age, Marketing Communications,* or *Sales & Marketing Management* will do much to generate awareness of the author. In addition to those so-called horizontal publications that cover all areas of the marketing world in depth, there exists in each industrial group a series of its own vertically oriented—or specialized—publications. These periodicals solicit articles on specific topics of interest to its industry's readers and often have a marketing section or column. For the marketer involved, for example, in the area of soft-drink marketing, an article on the latest developments in either container design or transportation may be exactly what the editors of *Beverage World* are looking for. Marketers who are alert to the demands of the publishing industry for creative output that is consistent and pertinent to their readers' interests can early on cement relationships as contributing editors, which will begin to establish a meaningful identity for them. Many marketers, as they advance along the road to greater corporate responsibility, have found the world of so-called business books another avenue for impression making in the human resources market. For the marketer fortunate enough to be published in her own right, the rewards in terms of exposure and publicity will be obvious.

THE TEACHING
AND LECTURING SEGMENT

One of the most significant changes that has taken place in academic circles during the past ten years has been the trend toward reality in the classroom. Everyday practitioners of those various subjects that students, particularly at the graduate level, are studying have been finding their way into American universities with an accelerating rate of frequency. It is no longer the dictum "Do as I say" that distinguishes today's instructor, but rather it is her ability to bring to students learning from the field of actual experience that holds forth as the preferred method of instruction. Marketers who are sage enough to have thought through their own marketing techniques in a formalized manner, so that such techniques can serve as substance from which a course can be developed, will find that there is a ready market for their services in the classroom. Such lecturing opportunities and seminar participation are a major source of exposure for the talent category of merchandise that is constantly being viewed in the human resources marketplace.

INFORMATION TRANSMITTAL

Among the five segments that have been identified as those critical for penetration in the human resources marketplace, a cross-referencing of information gained from one to the other is a subtle but telling part of the market functioning. Though perhaps seemingly unrelated, there exists a core number of participants in each of these five segments who perform the function of passing the information gathered along from one segment to another. It is actually the business of this group of personnel— those who will be in attendance as core members of each of the groups— to transmit valuable personnel intelligence from one group to another. As an example, an editor at a prestigious trade journal may have her or his advice sought for a recommendation of several candidates for a seminar panel for a course in marketing being developed in a leading university. Writing or publicity skills demonstrated during the course of a charitable fund-raising campaign may earmark one for possible future recommendations as an article writer in a trade association journal issued annually on the occasion of that society's international conference.

At the highest level of each of the five segments outlined, there is a constant rating of those who participate and a ranking of them as against those who are just in attendance. This information is shuttled back and forth for the benefit of the greater good. The iceberg factor is always in operation. From a marketing point of view, the activity is the essence of that function known as cross-selling. What this means is that the benefits of selling oneself into one segment of the human resources market have extended value into all of the other segments. Once the first sale has been consummated, the "merchandise" will be on recommendation in other areas of the human resources environment. It is only a matter of time until the right customer will come along and complete the transaction.

DEVELOPING A POSITION
FOR THE PRODUCT

The analogy of marketing the marketing woman, as it is drawn to that process involved in bringing goods or services to market, employs the skills of positioning in just the same manner as they are applied in the nonhuman resources marketplace. As noted, the identification of the components of the marketplace is the first step. The second step involves directing and packaging the product—in this case, it is that person or persons who seek to have themselves consumed by one or more segments of the human resources market. If the positioning activity is to have its desired result, if it is to present a unique "product" suitable for filling voids or needs in the marketplace in a manner that is demonstrably superior to that of the other personnel products available for consumption, then certain key factors must be attended to. There are five that make up the personnel positioning process.

Skill Type

The essentials of one's primary areas of expertise are the primary benefits of the product that need to be communicated. The distinction as to skills—administrative, creative, financial, research, production, management, and the like—need to be communicated to these human resource influentials who will be following the market. These skills are analogous to the attributes that a package design will convey for the marketer of a consumer nondurable. They must clearly outline the category of product being offered so as to narrow, for the consumer, the area of interest and thus facilitate choice. The marketer who presents herself as a generalist, when indeed her outstanding skills may well be in the new-product-development area, will do no more than present a blurred and confusing image. Positions must be clearly defined if they are to penetrate to the needed side of the human resources purchasing process.

Being of a Career Mind

No single factor can be more damaging to the woman marketer who seeks visibility as she builds her early career asset base than the absence of a clear-cut impression that she is in the business world for the purpose of seriously pursuing a career, as contrasted to the objective of holding down a job. The influentials in the human resources market have little interest in identifying short-term work aspirants. Rather, they seek to focus their attention on that woman who demonstrates her sincerity of purpose in making those sacrifices that will single her out as being in the human resources marketplace for the long term. Simple economics guides this consuming philosophy. There is a negative financial trade-off involved in an investment of corporate assets, and they are considerable, in the development of executive marketing talent whose span of career activity is obviously to be limited. The human resources market is judicious in the placement of its investments and seeks the maximum period of time over which to have them bear interest.

How to Facilitate the Purchase

The final step for the woman marketer, who will want to cement all her armaments for maximizing her career potential, will lie in the difficult area of making the sale. No technique is better suited than that which sets up an apparatus that can be used and built, and added to, over the long term. It is an apparatus that the woman marketer should always have in place. It is an apparatus that is most like the sales arm of a marketing organization. Such an apparatus will allow the woman marketer to make her availability as an active pursuer of either career change or career ascendancy known to those buyers in the human resources marketplace who will be continually consuming. It is a mechanism that relies on the need to feed information about career opportunities to the woman marketer and also to feed information about her availability to the consuming sector of the marketplace.

Networking

Women have come to realize that given their late start in the marketing world, they have had little opportunity to develop the "you scratch my back, I'll scratch yours" technique. Known as networking, it has been at the core of male career change and job ascendancy for centuries. Women need only to read those statements of corporate leaders that daily find their way into the business press and attesting to their inability to find suitable female candidates to fill major posts within the organization. This is not mere rhetoric on the part of chauvinistically inclined male management, but rather a fairly accurate evaluation and appraisal of a market situation in which women have not been in the positions and have also not had the inclination to be chauvinistic about recommending and taking care of their own. The woman marketer who looks for the long-term gain will do well to establish her own network in the corporate world. Women, notwithstanding the quasi-democratization of the boardrooms of America, will do well to join in partnership with other women who have made it in the marketplace. Building such a network and assuming the attitude that a female-directed quid pro quo position is a legitimate weapon for the career-minded woman—all other things such as competence and commitment being equal—is a realistic and legitimate technique. In every sense of the word, it does justice to those basic techniques of marketing that seek to maximize whatever extra benefits are available to a product as it competes for a share of the market's dollar expenditure in competitive environments.

All Roads Lead to an Interview

Although this chapter is directed toward establishing self-marketing techniques that are presumed to be of use in the future, no review of such an approach would be completely useful without addressing the all-important question of tactics employed by the marketer who will one day actually be faced with making a career change. Considerable data exists with respect to career-changing techniques. Again, the analogy to the marketing philosophy is helpful. Career changing does have within it the components of art and those of science which this book maintains are essential for understanding marketing's true function. Methods for getting the most out of job interviewing follow this same part art, part science formula.

MANAGING A DIFFICULT PERSONNEL SITUATION

The marketer's skills, the full arsenal of personal and intellectual talents, will be called upon in handling the job interview process. So much is nebulous and so much subjective in this institutionalized process known as the job interview that only a professional approach to making the most of it seems worthwhile. From actual experience as both an interviewee and interviewer, I will attempt to outline broad areas of concern which, if attended to, can help the career-bent marketer in her search for a better work life.

TAKE COMMAND.   In an interview situation, the implicit character of the meeting places the applicant on the defensive. She is being shopped; she is not really the shopper. It is desirable, therefore, to take control of the conversation and to seek to guide it in several directions.

SHOWCASE THE PRODUCTS—YOU!   Direct the conversation to areas of your own special competence, to which you can present supporting data as proof positive of accomplishment.

AVOID THE BEGGING SYNDROME.   Be direct in avoiding the superior-subordinate relationship. Your presence in an interview does expose a need-filling situation, so there is no need to be defensive, submissive, or otherwise too anxious.

CONFORM TO THE NORM.   Avoid positioning your accomplishment or personality type as different from what the standard corporate image is at any one prevailing moment in time.

INVOKE CUSTOM TAILORING.   Seek to reduce the unknowns in the interviewer's description of what he or she is looking for. Marketers would do well to zero in on the specifics of the job description and tilt the presentation of their own qualifications in that particular area.

MAKE PERSONAL CONTACT.   The most professional of interviewers are, after all, humans and can therefore be appealed to in areas that touch them. An acknowledgment of this human factor will direct the career-changing marketer to those personal areas of interest, whatever they may be, to which sincere attention to commonly held attitudes can be keyed. If the marketer makes personal contact, the entire interview situation will be more comfortable for both participants.

DON'T BE AFRAID TO ASK.   There are logical questions that will be in the marketer's mind. They run the gamut from the nature of the reporting process to salary, promotional opportunities, the nature of turnover in the organization as a whole, and the specific job situation that is being discussed. Intelligent and tactful probing serves to display the assertiveness of the marketer and allows the interviewer to assess the level of preparation the applicant has undertaken in researching the background of the company she presumably wishes to work for.

HAVE VIABLE ANSWERS.   Inevitably, the career changer will be asked a host of questions with regard to her personal and professional life which must be answered. The test in this case is to prepare for such questions in advance and have forthright, personally flattering answers available. Such questions can run the gamut from why the applicant seeks to change jobs (a good answer is for greater salary and responsibility) to a probe as to those areas in which the marketer feels she is least capable.

The final step in the interviewing process is the follow-up. This is best accomplished in a letter that restates the reasons why the applicant is interested in the situation and feels she is best suited for it. Follow-up phone calls are also in order. The rules of the interviewing game presume a certain etiquette, and the applicant who recognizes that she is entitled to an answer to her investment in time and effort in the job-search function will be respected.

Marketing the marketing woman is a subtle process that can be mastered. Unfortunately, in the rush to perform on the job, many women marketers will have neglected this important area of career development. As techniques become increasingly more formalized, the astute marketer will do well to reread this chapter. Though only the fundamental, broad areas of building an asset base for future utilization have been covered, the insights will nonetheless be valuable.

15

Looking and Acting the Part of the Executive

America is the land of the free and the home of the executive. If the French can be said to govern by means of a well-structured administrative bureaucracy, the English by the delicate balancing of the monarchy with the private sector, it's realistic for the woman in marketing to recognize that executive status in America is very much our form of aristrocracy. This country, in response to its preeminent personality as a business-driven society, has for all intents and purposes invented the executive.

A quick look at the trappings and vocabulary of our culture support this point. We have keys to the executive dining room. The upper reaches of a corporation are referred to as the executive suite. The distinction in corporate organizational charts is made as to who is the chief executive officer. In our local, state, and even federal governments, the influence of the business-trained executive can be felt. One recent high-level cabinet officer came to his secretarial post directly from the chairmanship of a major industrial corporation. The second-in-command of one of the country's largest publishing enterprises now advises the president on matters of policy. Another from the ranks of the management consulting industry gives advice on executive style and attitude, including such things as work hours, efficiency, paperwork management, and the like. Ours is a country of managers, whose aspirational levels are constantly directed toward leading and supervising. Major brokerage houses, retailing establishments, and business schools all have courses of training referred to as executive training programs. The focus is on developing future executives. One can also pay for and attend various schools and seek out counselors who promise to help develop executive skills and talent. There is even a distinction made at the secretarial level. Presumably the executive secretary has more skills, better pay, and a chance at true executive leadership than a woman who simply types for a nonexecutive manager. The emphasis on this aristocracy goes on and on. The job seeker is advised to develop an executive resumé. *The Wall Street Journal* attributes a great portion of its annual advertising revenues to its Positions Wanted and Positions Available Executive Mart classified advertising pages. The point is made. In the land of the executive, one must know how to look and play and cope with the role. It is simply not enough to be competent and to perform. There is an entire series of accessories, if you will, that go with the basic outfit.

ATTIRE

Though a previous chapter has indicated that too much can be made of this, the realistic outlook is for the woman marketer to view her appearance as a cosmetic gesture that will affect some people. Conservative is the key word. Your clothing and the way you present yourself make a statement about you. A conservative approach is seen as a competent approach, and that's what the business world wants. It cannot take revealing, tight-fitting, suggestive clothing. For the sharp business woman, the correct appearance spells profit. Those who would overdo makeup, fragrance, and the like certainly call attention to themselves— but for all the wrong reasons.

Common Sense: Use it!

Clothes may not make the woman, but negligence in attention to the simplest of things can do much to unmake her. There are certain pitfalls you can avoid by recognizing that you are on display in the business environment. Being an executive is a twenty-four-hour-a-day undertaking. Your habits should reflect this.

1. The woman executive must always look the part. It can be embarrassing to walk into an office and find the receptionist wearing the same dress. The trick here is to stock your wardrobe with a few good, expensive items rather than a broad range of different, less expensive outifts. If your budget is limited, this is very important. Also, you will

find the better clothes wear well and can withstand travel and rainy days and still look crisp after a flight or a day in a suitcase.

2. Dress your age. There is nothing quite so image-debilitating as a woman executive who has let the latest fashion trend carry her away. If blue jeans tucked into western boots are the rage, save them for weekends when you're with friends and can be casual in your attire and demeanor. And beware of the new-style skirts with so many slits that sitting becomes impossible. Save those for cocktail parties.

3. Travel in style. An airplane may be a singularly uncomfortable place to spend long periods of time in a skirt and heels, but you never know what important executive you may meet on the way to the sales meeting. Leave your jeans and tennis sneakers packed until you hit the courts. Find something comfortable and fashionable to travel in.

4. Avoid the "bag lady" label. Though you may well need to transport a returned item to a department store, stow your makeup and gym suit, and tote last evening's market forecast to the office on any one day, it's better to carry less than more. Try to limit your carrying habits to a handbag and briefcase. If it all gets too overwhelming, then try to manage everything in one giant tote. It's easier on you and easier on the eye. And tuck your morning paper in your briefcase so it won't protrude from under your arm.

APPROACHING OTHER PEOPLE

There is a very delicate shift in attitude that takes place once a person achieves executive status. The key word is *status*. It equals privilege and as such, must be treated with respect. No one enters the business world entitled to executive status; it is usually hard-earned. Misuse of it can be instrumental in the loss of it. Its power as well as its glory must be guarded. Much of a woman executive's time will be spent with other people. Executives are expected to lead and to motivate. In this regard, it is helpful to remember that you catch more flies with honey than with vinegar.

1. *Do unto others.* Be courteous. Just because you've had the good fortune to make it doesn't mean other people are not persons also. Don't flaunt your status for power's sake.

2. *Don't be a snob.* If yesterday you were in the typing pool and today you've been promoted to the sales force, that's no reason to forget all the people whose work and effort helped to get you there. You can expect to be treated as an executive—that is, you'll no longer be "one of the girls"—but make sure your former peers know it hasn't gone to your head.

3. *Your title.* It's wise to make certain you are called by your last name whenever possible. The familiarity of first names throughout the office is a mark that you are still among the group. This is one of the prerogatives of status. Use it, if possible. If your peers are called *Mister* and you don't follow suit, you will never be on the same level (psychologically) within the office environs.

4. *Don't blow.* No matter how provoking a situation or a person may be, never lose your composure. There is a time and place to rectify every situation. Displays of anger have the effect of frightening people and turning them off. Even though you may be in the right, the executive who makes the mistake of exploding in public will be seen as one whom the larger corps of followers will mistrust. There is nothing so unnerving to the corporation as a loss of faith in executive leadership. At best, it will foster an apathetic attitude on the part of other employees. At its worst, it will serve to sow dissension, intrigue, and disaffection with the rank and file. If you can't motivate in a positive manner, better to seek another area of employment. The organizational world is not for you.

The attitude and mind set that the woman executive brings to her responsibilities are important. Two factors have overriding importance: the first is the ability to bring a positive mental attitude to the job; the second is the interactive nature of the executive position. Both areas must be mastered.

HANDLING SUCCESS

The world is a difficult enough place in which to cope without compounding the difficulty by emphasizing what can't be done at the expense of what can be done. Most tasks are not as difficult as they seem, so it is wise to have a positive attitude. In this regard, much psychological study has been undertaken to define those things that condition such a positive attitude. Dr. Ari Kiev, author of *A Strategy for Success* (Macmillan Publishing Company, Inc., 1977) offers the following pointers:

1. To develop a positive attitude, look for situations in which your reaction is different from that of the mainstream. By so doing, you will be reinforcing your creative capabilities. It takes some imagination to be a positive thinker.

2. Observe how often you let others think for you. Avoid it. If you've got a point of view, don't be easily dissuaded.

3. Don't seek the permission of others on routine matters that you can handle yourself. Many times this form of "covering" will be that and that only. An attempt to spread the blame for a certain course of action fails.

4. Be modest about both your successes and failures. Overemphasis of either can brand you as an incompetent or a braggart. Critically, an emphasis on failure (we all fail at one time or another) is highly destructive to a positive mental attitude.

5. Enhance your spirit of adventure and discovery. Trying and succeeding at new things affords the woman marketer the opportunity to avoid boredom, take risks, conquer stress situations, and develop hidden talents.

6. Do it now. A sense of accomplishment is the best medicine for the ego that may be on shaky ground. If you can handle tasks as they arise during the course of the work day, you will see results on a continuing basis. Such constant reaffirmation of your skills and your worth are supportive.

7. Learn how to ask pertinent questions and how to listen. Positive attitudes depend in good measure on information and knowledge. You cannot bluff a positive approach to business. So take every day and every personal contact as an opportunity to educate yourself.

8. When looking back at mistakes you have made, try to position your attitudes so that you can confront such situations again and master them.

Thinking the Part of the Executive

To the extent that your attitudes and general approach to business—your executive style, if you will—is affected by your thinking and point of view, this corollary to looking the part of the executive is very important. It has within it particular significance for women. Women's relative newness to the executive world provides them with a rare opportunity to have themselves heard and their influence felt—an opportunity that is seldom presented on such a scale.

DON'T BE AFRAID TO THINK LIKE A WOMAN.   The manager of the future will be beset with a host of problems her forebears hardly dreamed of. It is anticipated that the continued growth of the technological bias will make the work environment one in which the manager of the future will have to cope with an increasingly restive work force. The depersonalization of the job, the breaking down of efforts into ever smaller and smaller components, promises to leave the work force without an understanding of where they fit in and what merit their own contributions have. Such an environment is an ideal breeding ground for apathy, lethargy, narcissism, connivance, power base accumulation, and destructive competitive activity. The responsible woman executive will see this future and develop primary skills with which to deal with it.

A HOUSE DIVIDED.   As the sage Lincoln said, the family (country), group, or work force that is divisive in nature will ultimately fail. Management according to the fear principle will get results for a time, but if applied over the long haul, it will foster an apathetic work attitude. Far better the executive who can motivate in a positive manner so as to get the group going toward a commonly agreed-upon goal and then look to natural momentum—the efforts of the self-starter, which can be developed within all of us—to carry the ball.

LOOK FOR THE RIGHT LANGUAGE.   "Please" and "thank you" go a long way. It is amazing what the proper attitude toward people will do, and in this respect, the little things count. Who would have imagined the accomplishment of mutual self-sacrifice on the part of lending banks, the government, management, stockholders, and union personnel a few short years ago? This mutual sacrifice has kept the Lockheed Company and, more recently, the Chrysler Motors Corporation in business. An executive can never expect to enter into such dialogues with different elements of a company's structure unless the sincerity of his or her language reflects the sincerity of attitudes. Women executives will be working with a better-educated work force. At this very moment, American college campuses have room for upward of 10 million young men and women. They are exposed, they are literate, they are informed, they are conditioned by the effect of one ill-conceived war, one fallen-from-grace President, and the specter of less of the good life. They are further conditioned by a strong egalitarian movement in the social structure. Minorities of color, race, and religion are fully a part of the fabric of American life. It will be incumbent upon the woman executive to learn their languages, to motivate rather than patronize, to ask with authority rather than decree and lecture, to criticize with constructive suggestions, to recognize that without followers the executive's role is removed from the organizational chart.

DON'T OVEREMBRACE THE MALE MODEL.   Having very few from her own sex to look to, the woman executive is most naturally given to emulate the executive style of men. Men have set the standards. Just remember that not all of them have been effective standards. Women tend to outdo in degree those things that their more savvy male peers recognize as counterproductive. There is no excuse in saying one is simply doing what men have been doing for years. Look at the situation yourself and find new solutions. Men have no corner on the behavioral techniques of the market. A fresh look is always better than blind adherence to methods that have been in place, and probably unreviewed, for years. Be skeptical about set-in-place executive techniques. If they are truly effective, they will stand up to your scrutiny. If they suffer under dissection, then it is time to make some changes.

DIALOGUES.   Two-way communication is the essence of productivity and innovation. The open environment acknowledges that each participant in the work force can, if he or she is so inclined, make personal points of view known. The wise executive, regardless of the corporation size, will be certain that there is a mechanism for doing this and a spirit that stands behind such forums. Dresser Industries, a multibillion-dollar industrial giant with both domestic and multinational investments, recognizes this need for the dialogue. Its formalized worker-supervisor-executive human resources program is an ongoing one. The company's management philosophy is summarized in a policy statement entitled "Teamwork and Technology." There is an acknowledgement at every level of the company that no man or woman is an island. Each worker is to some extent and in some manner dependent upon the efforts and goodwill of another. Various company divisions are urged to be familiar with all the company's other divisions. Compatibility and communication are the key words. The Dresser credo is summed up in a few words: "Machines and personnel are our only assets."

THERE WILL ALWAYS BE THAT ONE PERSON.   Notwithstanding the efforts of enlightened managements to nurture and develop a spirit of cooperation, experience suggests that having to cope with that difficult personality will be a task the woman executive will most certainly encounter. The rule of the road in such situations is not to avoid that person, but to limit one's contact as much as possible. Keep to the book—that is, do the job even though you might prefer a transfer or a different working partner. One need not be the best friend of another for meaningful work results to come out of such relationships.

ONE OF MANY.   The experience one encounters in the family situation, where parents, various sibling and other extended members are in a constant state of interaction, will serve the woman executive well in the larger corporate family. Executive thinking, which recognizes the need for a balance in the demand and attention paid to the requirements of any one person, is on-target thinking. All of our actions have an effect, either directly or indirectly, on all other persons in a work situation. Executives must appreciate that the needs of the group must always supercede the needs of the single individual.

PREDICTING
EXECUTIVE ACHIEVEMENT

I have previously indicated my bias against strict formulas and overly structured systems of thinking. It would, however, be a disservice to aspiring women marketers not to cover certain areas of scholarly research which for better or for worse have found some degree of acceptance in the general opinion-making area. Christopher Jencks, a Harvard sociologist, has recently published the results of his work, *Who Gets Ahead? The Determinants of Economic Success* (Basic Books). Certain predictable criteria are outlined. The author emphasizes the broad interpretive nature of such works. They are, at best, clues based on the accumulation and interpretation of large amounts of data. They describe in a very broad manner a general profile of the successful executive. Their utility lies in recognizing realities about executive life in America, and also in providing broad guideline to the thinking of senior managers who run and make the hiring and firing decisions at most major corporations.

Checklist for Determining Executive Success

Jencks has outlined eight key factors that affect the win-lose ratio in an executive career. Be honest with yourself in evaluating these factors.

1. Test scores play an important part. Though some women will not test well—that is, the stress encountered in the test situation is too much for them—by and large, these women manage to overcome this debility and show from an early age (sixth grade) the ability to score well on achievement and aptitude tests, satisfying the first criterion of executive achievement.

2. Length of attendance at a school counts for little. What does count is that all-important degree—the college degree—which is a license required for executives who wish to get ahead.

3. It is not so much what you actually learn in school that counts as what you do with it. There are many knowledgeable persons who cannot make it in the executive suite because they fail to grasp the practical requirements of putting knowledge to work.

4.   There is no greater payoff for bright students than there is for those who are simply more persistent. Hard work counts.

5.   If you focus your thinking on high pay only, you will inevitably end up at the low end of the executive scale. Such myopic thinking tends to develop a one-dimensional personality. These people are ill-suited to the generalist demands of the contemporary business organization.

6.   Status and title can be misleading. They do not always lead to well-paying executive positions. A title on the door does not always mean more money. Too often it is a cosmetic gesture.

7.   Personality traits are equally important as test scores in predicting status and earnings. Naturally, the leader personality will do best.

8.   Family background does play a part, though there will always be that first-time person. The woman who comes from a background within which executive status and the dynamics of executive thinking and executive perspective are given will have an edge.

The realistic opportunities women can look forward to in the executive management levels of various corporations do, of course, have a direct relationship to the amount of remuneration they can expect to achieve. Looking and acting the part of the executive, thinking the part of the executive, being an executive twenty-four hours a day, should be both a personally rewarding and fulfilling experience as well as one that will allow for the accumulation of certain monetary rewards.

IT PAYS TO HAVE
A PHILOSOPHY

There is every bit as much a life-style that can be said to be the executive's as are those life-style labels that are attached to the person who chooses the arts or the professions for her life work. The executive philosophy devotes its energies to the propagation of the business organization as the most important factor, after family and self, in one's life. The demands are constant. Recent studies among executive women indicate that if a choice between career and personal life were to be called for, then the demands of family, personal life, and children would not be sacrificed. They are the preeminent considerations for most women. It requires a shaping of one's attitudes to allow for the intrusion of executive life to the point where it can be seen for what it is, what its rewards are, and what its heavy burdens and responsibilities are. Workers will be dependent upon the decisions of executives.

Quite literally, the bread that enters the mouths of those who you will direct rests upon the accuracy of your judgment and actions. Feeling this responsibility is part of the executive look I refer to. Candor and truth, sagacity and maturity will be called for. The woman who would look and act the part properly will soon find that the look transforms itself into a total approach. Once this plateau is reached, the likelihood of success and fulfillment will be nearer to reality.

V
SPECIAL CONSIDERATIONS

16
A Business of Her Own

In the late 1950s, a then-Secretary of Defense in the post-Korean War days of a rather listless economy noted, to his eternal embarrassment, that "what is good for General Motors is good for the country." The gentleman's embarrassment was caused by his own previous proprietary relationship with that economic colossus, which has indeed provided considerable stimulus to the American economy, as have its counterparts in the sector known as big business.

Large corporations constitute a significant portion of that figure referred to as the gross national product. To lend some perspective to the dimension of their contribution, it is sufficient to note that the annual sales of several of the nation's largest corporations, by themselves, exceed the gross national product of several of the smaller emerging nations. There is no question about it, big business is big business.

The consternation generated by Mr. Charles Wilson's remarks had not so much to do with dissenting views as to the true contribution of the large corporation (this would seem to be indisputable) as it did with something else. What bothered Mr. Wilson's critics was the implication that only big business had a significant hand in the management of the American economy. What this gentleman had unwittingly done was to throw down the gauntlet and insult the entrepreneurial spirit of countless thousands of Americans who prided themselves on their own self-employment. It was as though a very basic right of freedom had been eliminated, and no less the same spirit of aggressive pride prevails today.

The small, independent, individually owned proprietorship, that entity referred to as "your own business," is alive and well and no doubt under active consideration by many readers. In a day when the strains of economic freedom impinge from every corner of the land, when government regulation would seem to be everybody's nemesis, and the paperwork nightmares of various federal, state and municipal legislative and administrative bodies cause the individual operator to wonder when he or she can get down to what they are in business for, this continuing urge to own one's own is indeed a wonder.

A look at the statistics reveals just how significant a force the small or independent business woman or man is. There are approximately 11 million nonfarm businesses in this country. By federal government standards, 10.7 million are small enterprises; they account for 58 percent of private sector employment. In terms of dollars, the contribution of persons who own their own businesses or work for independent business to the GNP is estimated to be about 43 percent.

The impact, therefore, of those persons who choose to become self-employed is obvious. For the woman in a marketing situation, the motivations that lead to ownership and the methods that can be utilized from the marketer's present training are vital first steps, should the process that often starts with a casual thought that one can do better on one's own already be an active consideration.

FACTORS UNDERSCORING THE INDEPENDENT BUSINESS OWNER'S PHILOSOPHY

For women, now emerging as such an important force on the economic scene, the processes that lead to striking out on one's own are probably more distilled and specific than they are for men. The fervor that underscores freedoms sought by the women's movement raises these causative factors more readily to the surface than they had previously been. Additionally, women as a whole are highly motivated by success as it relates to their accomplishments. Hence, they are easier to identify and examine. These motivations are an interrelating group of psychological and practical drives, some of which are examined from a very practical viewpoint by these participating women, and others which are the result of more subtle and deep-seated factors. Given this unique opportunity, the underlying motivations—those psychological and those practical—are examined.

Independence

As a natural outgrowth of women's general emergence from a secondary position, the desire to be one's own woman is a natural motivation for those who seek to own their own businesses. That need to express oneself, free from the rules and regulations of corporate life which place a premium on conformity and that thing referred to as incorporating the norm within oneself, is a vital force.

Challenge

The risk/reward syndrome involved in the chancing of assets in a new business venture is considerable. The chances of failure are significant. The development of the instinct that leads one to take a chance, driven often by no more than a feeling, a hunch, an intuitive perception that one may prevail, plays an important part in the process involved in stepping out on one's own. The essence of this gambling instinct is the need to meet the challenge and undertake the game. It is a compulsion that operates at a higher or lower level of frequency within the personality of the risk taker. Though there is a careful appraisal of the odds prior to taking the plunge, the gambler will more often than not be driven by the hope of extreme or unusual gain. The gambler as a businessperson sees the continual accumulation of dollars as a prize worth chancing.

Entrepreneurial Thinking

For those women who find the pressure to conform toward the prevailing consensus on any one matter a difficult task, the opportunities that a business proprietorship offer are tempting. The distinction between the woman who holds entrepreneurial attitudes or opinions and the personality traits of the radicalized person is important to grasp. The entrepreneur will usually have a more creative outlook and skills. Her charge is to see if there is a better or different way to accomplish some task. Her nonconformity is entrepreneurial in that its objective is a better product, cheaper method of manufacture, more efficient sales plan. Achievement in terms of sales and profit growth are the object of her nonconformity. There is a method to her madness. The radicalized personality, on the other hand, is not one usually suited for entrepreneurial tasks. Her motivations are disruptive per se, and all too often have a greater ultimate impact against side issues in the business environment.

Though such women may see themselves as innovators, the

effect of their actions is usually directed to activities that are tangential to the basic profit motive of the individual business proprietorship.

Special Skills

Closely linked to the nonconformist factor is that motivation of the creative personality that seeks a free and unfettered structure for her work environment. The artists, writers, and graphic designers whose work is a style and personality extension of her own taste often find great difficulty in attempting fulfillment within the confines of structured corporate life. Notwithstanding the contemporary corporation's desire to provide the proper nurturing environment for such persons, they often find the ability to do their own thing a prime requisite of a productive work situation. The woman who is creative, who has these special skills, is a strong woman. She feels that she has something unique to say. It is her belief in her ability to create that is important to her. For her, an awareness that she is able to do a thing, which we call her special skill, ranks equally with her desire to have the dollar rewards of her work accrue to her alone.

PSYCHOLOGICAL
AND PRACTICAL FACTORS
TO CONSIDER

Tradition

Notwithstanding the current trend to downgrade tradition in some circles, no doubt because of the negative impact certain traditions have had within our social structure (for example, the secondary status of certain minorities, and the like), the force of tradition as it affects women in the choice of an entrepreneurial career as contrasted to a corporate career is significant.

The affect on personality development and therefore upon the choice of a business career that is felt by that person who grows up in a family unit in which the tradition of individual ownership has been well established, can be telling on the career path of the woman who chooses the business world. A successful father or mother may seek a better life for their offspring, one that is less tedious and more secure than the life offered to the entrepreneur, but often such admonitions do little to dissuade the maturing children. What is telling is the attitude of independence, there for the child to see, that affects the ambiance of the household. The growing daughter will quickly recognize that her mother or father is that thing referred to as a "boss." She will assimilate an attitude that from her earliest days emphasizes independence and self-reliance. At the dinner table she is more than likely to study the mechanics of business, being exposed at an early age to the fundamentals of owning one's own business: finance, worker productivity, sales, and the management of others, legal matters, taxes, and the like. The tradition of owning one's own business may very well be said to be in one's blood.

Though circumstances and special talents may dictate a different field of individual ownership and pursuit than the one engaged in by predecessors, it is the spirit and tradition of working for oneself that will often carry over from generation to generation.

Career Block

The continual demands of its career executives plays a key role in the process of making the decision that leads to individual proprietorships. The circumstances of being passed over for promotion or finding oneself in a safe but no-ascendancy position within the corporate pecking order is a factor that must be dealt with. Age, ability, the demands of one's family for a certain standard of living all come into play at prescribed periods during the executive's life. Usually, the man or woman who does not see or is blocked from that promotion that will vault her into the senior levels of the company she works for will consider the alternate direction of individual proprietorship. At this stage, the executive has often accumulated all those skills necessary for running a business, especially if she has progressed to a fairly high level of mid-management participation. Her contact base in her industry is extensive, and she has been able to make herself visible enough so that new business development efforts on her part have a fair chance of success. The blocked career is often the last straw in persuading the person who has often considered but never yet taken that final step to career independence.

The Take-Charge Syndrome

Certain dominant personality types have an innate ability to motivate, persuade, lead, and, in many circumstances, dominate people and situations. This person actually finds it almost impossible to subordinate herself and her wishes to the order and management dictates and techniques of the corporation. She is a very practical woman who knows exactly what she wants out of life and, more often than not, just when she wants it. Such women do well in business organizations of their own because they blossom when calling the shots. These are extremely strong personality types. They see a career as an employee more as an extension of academic training, on-the-job experience, than as a career opportunity. Their focus is to learn the maximum about business that their jobs will make available to them and to utilize this knowledge as a springboard to a business of their own.

Life-style

A combination of special attitudes has developed with amazing intensity in the past ten years, one which has sought to explode the proposition that big is necessarily better. There is a growing conviction among many women that less is indeed more. The true focus of such social attitudes has to do with the impersonality of corporate life on the one hand, and the belief that it is impossible to manage, no less guide, one's own fate within the larger, unwieldy corporate structure. Added to such factors are the practical demands of time on the new women's life: time for child rearing, time for a well-rounded personal life, time to enjoy the fruits of her labors. Though an individual business ownership will probably make more time demands on the woman marketer than a career within an organization, it is the management of her own time, now in her hands, that affects the business of her own decision-making process. Individual entrepreneurs are able to bend the time demands of life in such a manner so as to suit them best. It is their inner clocks that call the tune, not some impersonal corporate timetable or calendar. And one final factor has weight, and it is a very practical one indeed. The remnants of male dominance still hang heavily over the corporate world, ranging from sexual pressures on the job to less-than-equal opportunity. These attitudes can be critical in pushing the woman who is teetering on the brink of a business of her own off in that direction.

ANYONE CAN START A BUSINESS: NOT EVERYONE CAN RUN ONE

The woman marketer seeking to start a business of her own enters an area of the unknown. Wise marketers make every attempt to reduce the risk factor; not the least of their areas of interest are those having to do with the techniques of structuring a business. It is acknowledged by certain experts in the field that basic differences exist between that entity known as a small business and the management of a large enterprise. Nonetheless, certain parallels can be drawn, and none more clearly than in the area of fundamental business practices. As one might expect, those areas of business that corporate experience leaves only to a very few are the areas in which the first-time business owner will have to concentrate her initial efforts. These fundamental business skills are efforts undertaken long before an actual open-for-business posture can be assumed. An outline and appraisal of them includes capitalization, equity, compensation, division of responsibilities, legal ramifications, basic accounting procedures, and product or service pricing.

Capitalization

The success or self-sustaining curve of most new business enterprises will usually follow a route of slow and steady ascendancy. It is the experience of most new entrepreneurs that reaching that point of self-sufficiency can take longer than an original estimate would indicate when the sales figures exceed on a fairly constant basis the costs of doing business. The collection, formation, and subsequent application of capital—in the form of cash, physical assets such as office furniture and equipment, and other capital tools such as key personnel—are the first requirements of the fledgling business. Proprietors who are realistic in their end objectives seek to plan adequately for such investment.

Equity

The direct fruits of one's labor will, over the long term, return to the individual entrepreneur essentially in the form of wages and salaries and that thing called equity. This is the ownership factor in any new business. Equity, expressed in the form of stock ownership in a business, is a reflection at an in-going point in time of the stockholders' financial investment in the business. It is a guarantee of certain proprietary assets of the business which is binding over the long term. Equity usually reflects the leadership of the business; it can be said to be the controlling vote or factor in supporting those decisions made or taken by the principals of the business that will guide it for the long term. Equity further assures the investor of a certain degree of flexibility with regard to his or her own liquidity, for it can usually be sold, borrowed against, or otherwise used as an asset.

Compensation

Initial stages of new business development often place a premium on the utilization of cash. Until such time as the new concern is a going concern, many marketers choose to limit their own personal compensation. Instead, they nurture the cash needs of the business. Dependent on their ultimate objectives, and excepting those entrepreneurs who seek to maximize the ability to live off a business—that is, to withdraw more in salary and wages than the norms of profit would suggest—the agreement by principals in specific levels of compensation, and the establishment of specific time frames and ground rules for the management of such compensation, is a critical area of the going-into-business condition.

Division of Executive Responsibilities

Even for that woman who will be the only employee of a new business, the desirability of spelling out the job functions of the participant or participants is an important first step. For the single proprietor, the development of a job description serves the purpose of formalizing a set of priorities, thus giving some minimal degree of structure to even the smallest of businesses. Where more than one principal's time is under consideration, it will serve the new entrepreneurs well to determine and specify who is responsible for what. Such analysis of job function will formalize the working relationships, with the end objectives of clarity of purpose and maximum utilization of individual skills.

Legal Ramifications

New businesses have certain legal responsibilities that must be adhered to. The corporation as such is a responsible body, offering its owners both reward opportunities as well as certain specific liabilities that the law dictates. In a new business, prior planning should anticipate those ramifications wherein legal counsel can spell out the various do's and don'ts of business ownership and operation.

Accounting

The necessity to grasp and adhere to, at an initial stage of a new business's incorporation, the basics of a cost accounting system, offers the woman marketer perhaps the most significant weapon at her disposal to ensure the growth, safety, and success of her new business venture. The intricacies of cash flow, profit and loss, inventory control, financing, and the like, all must be mastered at an early stage. Of all areas in which the fledgling corporation will seek to husband financial resources, none is less likely to generate real savings than the skimping on professional accounting and bookkeeping services.

Pricing

The pricing of goods and services is, for the new entrepreneur, closely linked with the objectives of her overall marketing strategy and directly related to the realities of her day-to-day business operations, as outlined in the cost accounting system which she will institute. The marketer will recognize that the same facts that affect pricing decisions for the marketing of many products will affect her own directions. She must determine her price niche in the business area in which she will compete, the levels of pricing as available by the operations of competitors already existing, her long-term profit and growth goals. Will she, for example, be willing to buy her way into the marketplace by attractive initial prices, thus sacrificing shorter-term profits for what will actually be long-term investment purposes? Many new businesses choose this route. It is the focal point about which the emergence of Japan as a major industrial entity has been built.

Pricing considerations will also have to do with the basic and prevailing economic climate of the times. If the new business is a capital-intensive one—that is, one requiring long-term injections of cash to maintain inventory support and necessary personnel or to expand a capital base of manufacturing assets (plant and equipment)—then the pricing of goods or services should take this into account. The fundamental rule in adopting a pricing strategy is to view cash as a commodity for which a price must be paid. It is also to be viewed as a commodity that can earn interest by investment, at greater or lesser risk levels. Added to this will be the desire to build a new and self-owned business. Somewhere in the mix of these three factors, with the demands and realities of competitive pricing taken as a given, the individual proprietor will find a meaningful level of pricing that will give her the best chance to make her money work for her.

OPEN FOR BUSINESS

Inasmuch as the aspiring marketing woman now cast in the role of individual marketing entrepreneur will utilize the basic components of the marketing philosophy to formulate a marketing strategy for her new business, the task for initial attention will be that of choosing the strategies she wishes to follow. Here again, the elements of strategic planning and the development of a set of tactics will play a key role. And here again, the implementation of directions set down in a formal marketing plan will serve the new business owner well.

Plan Your Marketing Strategy

The choice of the proper strategy is totally dependent on the intended scope of service available for offering and the goals of the corporation. The new business owner should have the mission and the scope of the new enterprise clearly in mind. It is vital to be specific about what business you are in and what markets you are best advised to address your efforts to. For example, the marketing consultant will do well to set limits on the services she is best suited to offer. If strategic planning is her forte, then her offering literature will do well to zero in on this. If she has determined that her best competitive opportunity for the sale of such services exists in market areas that are underserviced or neglected as being too small by the new proprietors' larger competitors, then the direction of her selling efforts should be targeted to such peripheral or (for her) out-of-town markets.

A second factor in choosing the proper strategy for the new venture is a realistic appraisal of those resources such as special skills, manpower, materials, financing, and technology and productivity capabilities available to the new business for the accomplishment of strategic goals. A prospective client whose needs dictate the utilization of large numbers of headquarters personnel for the accomplishment of an administrative task that is key to their business development will be ill-suited to the prospect profile of the new entrepreneur whose limited financial resources will preclude the employment of large numbers of clerical personnel. The choice of a marketing strategy for a new business depends in the final analysis on the entrepreneur's ability to identify and satisfy needs in the marketplace. The new business that does not fully understand and accept the facts of life which support its conception and future existence is doomed to flounder and fail.

Go After New Business

Certain tasks of the individual proprietorships are distinct with regard to the emphasis placed on them from those the marketer would face in the in-place, going corporation. It can be assumed that the larger corporation has already survived the process of building its introductory sales base and is at the stage of concentrating its efforts on two other factors: product or market diversification activities and the management of all its physical and human resource assets so as to maximize the productivity of its undertakings. The same is not the case of the small business. The lifeblood of the new venture will be the rapid development of sales. All efforts will be directed to the exposure of the name, uniqueness of product or service, availability and competitive posture of the new venture, with the end purpose of writing business. Till such time as a sales base of customers is available, the emphasis must be to limit the long-term goals of planning operations, efficiency, and other managerial aspects of the business for the sake of sales development.

Tactics for New Business Development

The newly emerging business can benefit from the utilization of basic promotion techniques within the marketer's skill areas.

FREE PUBLICITY.   There is a considerable availability among local newspapers, trade journals, and targeted special-interest radio programming for the announcement that a new business has been established and is ready to service customers. A simple publicity release outlining the scope and mission of the business, its place of operation, and the names of key principals, usually with a listing of their former associations, is all the press will require.

DIRECT MAIL.   Where the profile of prospective customers is clearly defined, the new business operator can make a direct and no-waste, highly efficient approach to such organizations by utilizing the techniques of direct mail. Lists of such prospects are available through list brokers for a rental fee. An appropriate marketing piece and cover letter requesting an appointment for a presentation are often all that's needed to make the initial contact.

ADVERTISING.   To complement direct mail efforts, advertising in pertinent industry journals is also an effective method of producing visibility and awareness.
The primary facts of life with regard to generating awareness for the existence of a new business emphasize the selling process. It is the constant preoccupation of a woman entrepreneur starting out on her own. It may strain her natural capabilities in that she may be otherwise directed—that is, her skills may tend more to what is considered inside work. These women will have to adapt in the initial phases of business growth. The product to be sold is not so much the end of what she does as much as the nature, scope, and image of her business as a visible entity for consideration by the consuming segment of the market.

How to Secure Financing

An all-too-often sobering if necessary dimension of the new business process is added to the marketer's broad list of thoughts when the specter of financing—how to secure it—is considered. In this area, the limitation that society has traditionally placed on women requires remedial attention. Happily, it is now available.

The concept of borrowing per se has been anathema to most women prior to the time of the movement and its emancipating influence. The focus, as often mentioned, has been on the traditional verities of security. "Neither a borrower nor a lender be" might well be the credo that most influences women's approach to the subject of financing. New and much-needed light is shed on the matter by persons (women, in most cases) who are actively engaged in the financial community. Banks, insurance companies, and other lenders of equity and investment funds have recognized two primary factors that affect women's ability to finance new business ventures. These are the high level of professionalism and dedication of purpose that women, now given the opportunity, bring to the business world. Women have proven themselves to be competent at the process of making money and the networking systems, referred to in an earlier chapter. This emphasizes the sisterhood aspect of the business world as it is realistically constituted. Women in business are helping other women in business. They are hiring them and contracting for their services—in short, building a network of business alliances that seek to favor women wherever their competence levels are on a par with those of men.

THE FINANCIAL COMMUNITY'S ATTITUDE.   There is hardly a more conservative group of professional businesspeople than those who represent the interests of the financial community. These people traditionally view the process of lending money with a realistic eye toward minimizing risk. Their assessment that the woman as businesswoman is worthy of consideration has resulted in an active role by these institutions in the pursuit of local opportunities concentrating in the women's market. And the attitude of these financial institutions is very much in keeping with the myth-shattering, negative, traditional avoidance needs of the times. A recent statement by Ms. Pamela Flaherty of New York's Citibank places the financial community's point of view in perspective: "Debt is leverage—use someone else's money to increase your assets. . . . Debt is also a kind of enforced savings because you've got to make monthly payments, but don't borrow more than you can handle."

GUIDELINES FOR ESTABLISHING CREDIT.   There are certain accepted standards to be followed by the women contemplating the need, present or future, to borrow money for investment in a business area:

1.   To establish a financial identity in one's own name, not in the name of a spouse.

2. Follow the same procedure when establishing charge or credit card accounts.
3. Establish a credit line at a bank—borrow money and repay the loan—before the money is actually needed. The willingness to repay loans, however small, is one of the critical factors a lending institution will review when making the decision to grant or refuse a loan. As the Citibank executive went on to say, "Handling credit is a very precious thing."

Women marketers who are up to the challenge of beginning a business of their own will find the process one of the most demanding they can undertake. It is not simply a matter of determining that one has the motivation. It will be obvious from a review of any statistics that attest to the failure and attrition rate of new business in this country that the task is not for everyone. Notwithstanding the less-than-supportive statistical data, the fulfillment a sole proprietorship offers to women marketers demands consideration. It is a particularly attractive option if superior personal skills and talents are available and can be upgraded. It is a viable option for those seeking ultimate levels of control and, of course, for those seeking the benefit of unusual levels of financial reward.

17

Balancing a Career, Marriage, and a Family: How Possible Is It?

If I were to single out the one area of contemporary woman's life to which I think women would be well advised to pay the utmost attention as they contemplate career future, it is the matter of how to handle the various alternatives available—namely career, marriage, family, and various offshoots thereof. In the simple phrase, "If men were men, why not act like a woman?" I feel that I have both defined the problem and raised certain questions with regard to how to handle it successfully.

You will find this a complex but nonetheless do-able task. The key factor to be convinced of from the outset is that, like the question posed in the slogan, it is no simple task. Inasmuch as the balancing act comes about primarily as a result of the conflict that arises vis à vis marriage, an old institution, and women's careers, a relative newcomer, a look at the statistics will give you some perspective.

As of this day, only one third of American wives are busy at the work of being full-time homemakers raising children. Predictions indicate that by 1990 only one in four will be a full-time housewife and mother. The other three quarters of American married women with children will be devoting at least part of their efforts to career building and miscellaneous employment of one sort or another. The implications of these statistics are unmistakable. A radical transformation in the social role of women has taken place. With such activities bearing directly on women's lives, advice on how to cope with these social factors is important. Inasmuch as I have been in the vanguard group of this revolution, some tips derived from experience will be helpful.

I have, let me say at the outset, and I hope this will encourage you, recently celebrated my sixth wedding anniversary to a marvelous and caring man. That word *caring* is what I attribute our successful marriage and successful dual careers to. We have both made a commitment to a new day, and it is working for us. We have found tremendous satisfaction in being among the small group who have pioneered this new life-style. Though I will be quick to tell you that forging this new path has not always been easy, and that six years does not constitute an overly long track record, it's the only basis I have for evaluation! I feel an inner glow in knowing that for me, the best of both worlds' philosophy that career, marriage, and the family brings has been a tremendously rewarding and worthwhile experience.

A key fact I have learned is that this life-style is neither a total enhancer of the institution of marriage nor the thing that has destroyed it. What I think women will want to know most about are those methods I have found useful in making this life-style a workable one. Whatever your personal preferences are or will be, these hints should give you certain guidelines. I am not espousing one life-style over another. However, the alteration in our social, psychological, and sexual thinking has brought about radical changes in society. I feel it is my responsibility to tell you as best I can how you can cope with and manage these changes so that you will have the best chance to lead a personally rewarding and fulfilling life.

First, there are some basic points of thinking that must prevail if marriage, family, and career are to coexist. Chances are that your spouse thinks of his position on the work force as a career. Be sure that your position is viewed in the same light. If his is a career and yours is a job, you are already starting at a disadvantage. Those close to you must be aware that your career has the same importance to you and therefore is entitled to make the same demands on your time and energies.

Second, get rid of guilt feelings if the household chores are given a backseat. In an emergency, paper plates can replace the dishes you forgot to run through the washer, and a ten-dollar investment on your part for underwear can stall doing laundry for a day or two. There are weeks when nothing goes as planned. Be flexible, make sure your family is flexible, and most important, don't let spouse or children try to hang a guilt trip on you. Take a deep breath, think of *your* goals, and remember, "This too shall pass."

It will be obvious that the two-career family, as it emerges as the dominant fact of family life, will have an impact on every aspect of our society. Statistics on delayed marriage, lowered birth rates, and increases in the number of divorces are not idle playthings for demographers. They are simply society's way of confirming the trends of the new twentieth and twenty-first century life-styles. Beneath the demographers' patterns, certain key influences are at work.

The first influence, and a very important one, is the matter of human rights. And I am speaking of women's human rights. The age we live in has seen the most rapid flowering of worldwide, person-to-person human rights efforts in the history of man. At no time, with the possible exception of the American Civil War period when slavery was abolished, has the most consistent underlying force in the world been that which seeks to give the individual greater freedom of action and greater freedom to pursue her own individual goals. It is this urge to be free, more than any other factor, that has motivated the women's movement. And freedom has a price. In our society, one so classic in its devotion to the business ethic, freedom is paid for and women must buy it. Obviously, to purchase anything, you must have the cash. And how better to earn that cash than to work. It all fits into the tradition that has made our great country the marvel of the world.

As in most revolutions, this revolution of the human spirit has been a creative enterprise. A need to be free and equal has contributed to the invention of an idea that will have long-term benefits to the very economic system upon which our society is founded. Working women mean business. Business creates jobs. Jobs create payrolls. Payrolls are spent and goods purchased. Consumption increases and production must keep up. The role of the working woman is not only creative, it is expansive. As in any other newfound right or freedom, there is a distinction to be made between the responsibility that freedom or woman's human rights brings and permissiveness. As women, we have inherited the responsibility of making this newfound freedom work. And so we come face to face with the balancing act again. The manner in which one copes with the intricate task of balancing career and family responsibilities will, more than anything else, affect the long-term success and institutionalization of these hard-won human rights. In order to get a balancing act together, I suggest you follow me as I outline and discuss those broad areas you will want to pay attention to.

PRACTICAL ECONOMICS

It does not make any difference to women what the root causes of inflation are, or how successful or unsuccessful we may be in waging war against ever-increasing prices. The facts of life are such that unless we wish to enjoy a considerably lower standard of living than we have become accustomed to—that indeed women have contributed to—the two-family career income of real dollars is essential.

You will quite simply not be able to afford the cost of food, shelter, and clothing in the future unless you are part of a two-career earning situation. It is hardly a question any more of *should* one work, but rather the choice of which work women will pursue. Those things that you and your spouse or friend will want to share have gone and will continue to go up in price. One of the offshoots of women sharing career and family responsibilities is the expansion of the demand for goods and services. The working wife and mother needs far more than her stay-at-home counterpart. Wardrobes are required. The work situation demands it. Transportation needs expand as the commuter lines are filled with working women. The call for convenience foods expands, as does the demand for leisure activity, as women join the ranks of those who will purchase a vacation. The list goes on, and with this increase in demand, the consequences of more dollars chasing more goods makes for increasing prices. So fact number one, as you contemplate the balancing act, is a financial fact. Both you and your spouse will have to learn how to share the wealth and pay more for what you had individually purchased for less. The market has accommodated your entrance, and it's unlikely that you'll see prices come down.

TIME MANAGEMENT

For ages, women have been better suited than men to handle a wide variety of tasks that require short durations of time for completion. Count this as a skill that provides you with a major advantage. The work-home-child care syndrome depends as much on the proper management of time as anything else. You'll need to be an expert planner. Assuming for a moment that your child or children are cared for during the day, either at a school or by some outside person, you will have to budget your time carefully in order to attend to all that requires doing. Depending upon your financial circumstances, the task may be easier or harder. Naturally, anything you can afford to pay for will free your time for other activities. All the duties, responsibilities, and pleasures of your married career life are included in this time management effort. The net result will be a somewhat less spontaneous life, but perhaps a more rewarding one.

YOUR SPOUSE

The adjustments required of the husband of a full-time career woman should not be underestimated. I have found that the woman who has a caring man at her side has a big advantage in making the balancing act work. It is not only a matter of accommodating the sharing of duties which has previously been delegated to one sex or another that is at question. More important is the emotional commitment your spouse will bring to making the new life-style work. He must want your career success every bit as much as you do. He must realize that the fulfilled woman he loves depends on her wholeness and her identity as a result of achievements in the career field of her choice.

For the two of you it will be as though you are working at two jobs—yours and his, and vice versa, if the high-wire balancing act is to proceed safely. I reiterate, it is not easy.

A PAST/PRESENT PERSPECTIVE

The blending of career and marriage responsibilities represents a radical departure from the manner in which women have viewed their roles. In making the switch to today's life-styles, the transition will be a much more comfortable and smooth one if you maintain some of the perspective of the past. I feel that the easiest way to accomplish this is to avoid a complete turnabout in your approach to marriage and the family. What you will be experiencing, as I have, is an added burden in terms of time. You are the same woman you were, it is only the rationing of your time that will be different. Place your emphasis on getting the most out of the time available with your spouse and family. Live life on a qualitative, not a quantitative, basis. Don't alter your attitude toward love, child rearing, and the like just because your career makes additional demands. Instead, maintain those values and ethics of the past that you still find rewarding. Review your list and discard those things you no longer find rewarding. The fulfilled working mother is not like the modern artist whose only method of creation depends on a complete break with the past. Do this and you can rest assured that your marriage and all you hope for will be radicalized. Instead, I think you'd be wise to lean on tradition for whatever strength it can give you and then be creative and innovative about the future.

SHIFT GEARS FOR CHILDREN

Many women involved in the balancing act have fewer elements to manage than their sisters because they have made conscious decisions to either postpone or avoid the mother role. This is obviously a personal decision, one that you and your mate will share. It is really no one else's business. If this is the path you are contemplating, then obviously your marriage and career will have fewer demands placed on it. If motherhood is your thing, you would be wise to assess your particular work situation prior to starting a family. Many firms now allow women to work throughout their pregnancy, with a month or so leave time to get the baby settled in before returning to work. If these are your plans and the company goes along with them, it is manageable. If your firm is not so liberal, perhaps you would do well to look around for the type of firm that is. On the other hand, if you feel the need to take a long sabbatical to raise your children (three to five years), that's fine. Be aware, however, that you will probably have to start from square one when you return to the work force.

For the woman returning to the work force who has already given years to children's upbringing, the task is really the same, the only difference being that school-age children are less time-consuming and more self-sufficient than preschoolers. It is really a matter of psychological commitment more than anything else. There is no data available indicating that children of successful women are any less loved, cared for, or nourished than are those of full-time mothers. It is, however, your mind set that will count most. If you feel that children come first and career second in your hierarchy of psychological and emotional values, then stick to your guns. Chances are that if you are comfortable with yourself, your performance on the job will be a better one. And this is one of the main goals your balancing act is trying to achieve. Remember, it's a matter of individual choice.

With this major point, I hope I have given you a broad feel for what you should consider as you ponder the choice all of us have at one time or another been faced with. It is not an easy task and yet, as I have noted, it is do-able. Perhaps the best feel you can possibly get for this task that you approach is to listen to the tale of my own experience. I have devoted much time and effort to a careful analysis of the pluses and minuses of a career-marriage-family lifestyle, the costs and rewards involved for both myself and my family. I, of course, come down on the side of it all being worthwhile. And yet for you to decide, perhaps it will be easier if I let you peek over my shoulder as I describe a recent month in my life. Remember, I own my own business and am active in one of the most dynamic of all career fields, marketing. That is what it's like for me.

DIARY

During one recent month—or to be more specific, twenty-nine days—I managed to be at home with my family, sharing, for exactly twelve days. During that month, between my husband's out-of-town commitments and mine, each of us traveled a total of approximately 22,000 air miles. Though not all of you will have careers that call for so much out-of-town travel, the nature of today's marketing world is such that you may well be called upon to make several extensive trips a year. Should your job be in sales, you can of course count on much more than this.

Now, to get back to my month. If I recall correctly, I traveled to San Francisco once, twice to Chicago, and also to Tampa, Wisconsin, Denver, St. Louis, and twice to Cleveland. Since my home is on the eastern seaboard, the latter two trips were what I call one-day turnarounds. My husband and I were able to meet at home for dinner. During this twenty-nine-day period, I have packed and unpacked twenty-nine times, made twelve calls for advance hotel reservations, car rentals, and plane reservations, and talked to my travel agent a total of six times. These calls were usually for the purpose of trying to make last-minute arrangements and schedule changes in order to accommodate the changing schedules of my clients. I have eaten in hotel coffee shops five times, entertained clients at dinner four times, seen two airline movies, and caught up on my business reading and dictation.

Since I missed our anniversary, I sent my husband eight cards to compensate. I also made twenty-two calls either to his office or to our home, had three dresses cleaned, a pair of heels replaced, and recovered one lost overnight suitcase. I have also bought three ballpoint pens to replace those left on night tables. I have very definitely stayed away from the cocktail lounges of the hotels in which I stayed; I have driven across the Golden Gate Bridge and explored Water Tower Place in Chicago on a Saturday morning while staying over the weekend to be ready for a second client meeting. I have advised my husband via telephone how to launder underwear, how to run the dishwasher, and where to get the best price on disposable diapers. I have also had the good fortune to sit next to the senior vice-president in charge of sales for a major midwestern paper company who has since invited me to make a proposal to his corporation, swapped stories with three young women attending a fashion market in northern California, rewritten my speech for a sales promotion club, and wired my husband on his birthday. Obviously, during this period I've worked myself silly, but I love it. I have also had my share of guilty feelings, recriminations, longings to give it all up and settle down, and jealousy because I was absent from a long-anticipated social gathering, and angry about spending so much time away from my infant son.

This month, as I've noted, is not typical of what the married career woman will encounter. However, it is something she must prepare for. It is an accurate picture of what you may encounter. So you have to ask yourself two serious questions: Are the rewards worth the sacrifices, and will that all-important man in your life be able and willing to go along with it? Chances are if the answer to the second is yes, then as a career-oriented woman you will find that the answer to the first is also yes.

If your life-style is to be successful, both partners in the career marriage must above all be secure people. If you get nothing else from my discussion of the new life-style than an appreciation of this very important point—that it does take two special people to make it work—then I will consider my efforts a success.

Let's discuss for a moment, what I mean by singling out my secure husband as a source of encouragement and support for my efforts. How does one define this ideal spouse who above all is secure? How will you know the type when you meet it? Well, to start with, he will more likely than not be a pretty successful fellow himself. Strength has a way of seeking out others who are strong. It is a complementary action and an acknowledgment that the task at hand may be so difficult that the balance of two strong personalities will be required to handle the challenge. The man who is secure will not feel threatened by your competence.

Yours will not be a competitive business situation. Should you be the more successful of the two, it won't matter at all. The secure husband recognizes the different social, sexual, and business roles you each will play. If your life with him at home is what you as lifemates seek in one another, then it really doesn't make any difference who has just been promoted to executive vice-president. It's also more than likely that he will be a compassionate and understanding man. By that I mean he will be able to make allowances for the ground-breaking nature of the situation the two of you will find yourselves in and therefore overlook the inevitable tensions you will face along the way. More than likely, the secure man who will share your two-career marriage will be either a businessperson himself and thus familiar with the peculiarities of that special set of circumstances that go with being a businessperson, or he will have his life's work in a field very different from that of the world of commerce. If this is the case, he will most likely be fascinated with the goings-on in an area he knows little about, and again you will find your lives complementing one another. The sharing, caring husband of the career wife will be bold. There is a certain thrill that can only come in the process of discovery and adventure such as will characterize two-career marriages. It is a new path you will be leading, complete with all the excitement that special breed, known for its response to new challanges, possesses. Your spouse will be open-minded. He will have to ponder the implications of two sets of circumstance, his and yours. Before, it was only one predominant point of view that held sway. He will think of your career-marriage as being of the two of you, best characterized by the word we. And he will be wise and manly. For it will take every bit of that to make the career-marriage work. And men can do all these things.

And they can do them more easily than you might expect. No matter that the journey of women to pursue their basic human rights may not yet be all you might want it to be—you should recognize that the progress has not been achieved solely by women. Men of the younger generation have grown up with the freedom of the women's movement. To them it is a casual thing to share dormitories, vacation accommodations, weekend travel. To them the freedom of the civil rights movement and the antiwar impact, have been growing, everyday experiences. Quietly, perhaps haltingly, and at many times with a good deal of backsliding and less gallantry than one might hope for, many men, both young and old, have freed themselves from the traditions of the past to accommodate the new woman. Today men take the advent of career-marriage much more easily in stride. They are discarding the stereotypes of the past. Women and men have been growing into career-marriages as a natural evolution of the times. So the situation should become much easier.

No discussion of the modern career-marriage balancing act would, I think, be complete without a small discussion of vital and practical do's and don'ts. When all is said and done, it will be these things that get you through the day that really count.

A WARDROBE OF BALANCING ACTS

This is a short list of very practical things you can do to keep all the balls of the career-marriage act up in the air and rotating comfortably. It will take a little planning on your part. The ingenuity with which you accomplish these seemingly innocent tasks will go far to increase your rating with that man in your life.

The Contact Hour

Set aside a mutually agreed-upon hour of the day or night in which one or the other of you will make contact. If you are together at home, then choose whatever part of the day you like and devote the hour to your personal lives. By all means leave the office out of it, and forget household problems for the moment. You can go for a stroll, sit sipping coffee across the kitchen table, or what have you. The important thing to remember is that this time is for you. If you have children, do the same with them, but separately. And when you are separated, let the telephone be your contact bridge. There is nothing quite as reassuring as the sound of a loved one's voice when thousands of miles separate you. What you say will hardly matter. It is the gesture of making the contact that counts.

Plan Each Week

Precious time is what you'll have precious little of. So don't waste it repeating things like shopping and laundry each and every day. Organize your household with every bit as much effort as you would put into the creation of a marketing plan. If you can afford it, then you should have groceries, laundry, and the like delivered. If not, try doing one or two very large grocery shoppings in a month, filling in with staples as you need them. Try to set things in motion at the beginning of each week and then do as little as possible on the domestic side. Make your family time a sharing and enjoyment interlude.

Role Reversal

This trick doesn't have the ominous overtones the psychologists have given it. After all, if the fate of the nation depends on who takes the trash to the corner garbage can, you don't really have much of a basis for sharing anything. Try to divide the housekeeping chores. And try to have a night out with the girls once in a while. It will give you and your spouse each some needed privacy and will bring a stronger bond to your union.

Budget Review

Set your financial household in order so you come to think of your marriage as having only one breadwinner: the two of you. Set aside a special time of the month and forecast your income and expenditures for that period. Start the year off with an annual budget and then review it monthly. Your key to success will be in acknowledging that a career-marriage-family and a budget are operating in high gear when there is a fifty-fifty split of all assets.

Leisure

Once in a while, and I suggest you do this as often as possible, it is a good idea to forget the label of career-marriage. Forget the business world, yours and his, and simply get away from it all. Like the two lovers you were before this new life-style took over, just make believe that the world of commerce has stopped for a few moments, days, or as much time as you can manage. This will give you time to recharge your batteries. It will allow you to rediscover those wonderful qualities in one another that make this different and unique partnership work.

One final comment from a lady who looks enthusiastically forward to more of the same kind of years I have been enjoying in a full-time career-marriage-family. If you find that the costs of your new life-style are more than you had bargained for or can handle, then don't hang in there needlessly. Discuss the problems openly. Make whatever adjustments are necessary. Perhaps you will want to cut back on your work time and entertain a career that is less demanding. Perhaps he will be the one who will reduce his investment of time and effort in a career. Be frank with each other and make whatever adjustments are necessary to keep your union intact. I feel that in the long run, you'll most likely be better off for it.

A combination career-marriage-family are not for everyone, though they will be predominant. There is no shame in being part of that 25 percent of married mothers who in the final analysis will find their best careers taking place right in the comfort of their own homes.

18
Coping with Success

The entire subject of keeping some balance in one's life is of extreme importance to that woman who seeks to make the world of business her domain. Success can be a heady and problematic thing if there is no generally acknowledged set of criteria against which to judge it.

There is considerable irony in this situation, given the extreme difficulty that women have had in breaking through to the top levels of male-dominated organizations. The ground rules for coping with corporate achievement are well defined for men. Men have been conditioned, first and foremost, to expect success; they have been schooled since early years in those techniques that have become standards for handling whatever problems may arise in respect to the mantle of the winner which is cast upon them. Women have no such ground rules, and adopting those standards that work for their male counterparts is not as easy as one might imagine. Inasmuch as a woman's needs and attitudes are different, those standards cannot be transferred in toto. They must be sorted through, added to, and reworked within the sphere of woman's needs to integrate a career, marriage, and possibly family into one working unit. Till such time, if ever, that a comfortable balance can be struck, the needs to cope with success will supplant the more desirable need to enjoy it.

KNOWING SUCCESS WHEN YOU SEE IT

Oddly enough, the first problem women encounter with success is recognizing it. So conditioned to the ever-upward-climbing attitude that is the symptom of the overachiever, the successful woman will all too often keep herself too much involved with the detail side of her business. If, indeed, she does not herself recognize when she has arrived, much time and effort will be frittered away in keeping her finger in every pie. There is a time in the development of every business career when success is indeed achieved. The business will be reaching its monetary objectives. Long-range plans will be fulfilled, and a certain degree of comfort can be taken in the assurance that, barring unusual circumstances, something solid has been put in place. Though the successful woman may yearn for the romance of the start-up period, and even prefer its simplicity and personal-reward atmosphere to that offered by the condition of having made it, common sense and good business sense indicate that it is time to let go. When executive responsibilities and decision making can be, in part, delegated to others, the successful woman will recognize that there is a vast world as yet to be explored. Her best clue as to when she has actually arrived will present itself in the form of a look at other horizons to be conquered, other challenges to be met. That woman will have come into her own. It seems folly not to enjoy the fruits of such hard-won labor.

COPING: IT'S EASIER SAID THAN DONE

I would be less than forthright if I were to indicate that coping with success is not a task to be mastered. There are no quick fixes, and many a miss occurs along the way. Each of us has made her own choice in the matter. Each has weighed and evaluated those factors that are important. Money, if it is important, must be viewed as such. No need to be coy about it. Better to adopt the famous motto of the gentleman bank robber, Willie Sutton. After his twentieth incarceration for having made off with the entire cash receipts of some unsuspecting midwestern bank, he was quite up-front when asked why he kept on robbing banks. "Because that's where they keep the money," Sutton said. I think the point is made. Obviously, the demands of marriage, family if one chooses, and self-image are factors that must be dealt with also. What I suggest is that the strains of coping can be serious. And yet, if one thinks about them, plans for them, and is ready to deal with them, some sense of order and harmony can be achieved.

The need to master the success syndrome will not go away. A Scarlett O'Hara attitude won't help you to cope. Business organizations are coming into the arena with their own attempts at solving the problems. This is a positive sign. Forget, for a moment, how difficult a task it has been to get them to this level. Maternity leave without job jeopardy, child-care centers, and other such gestures are just the beginning of the corporation's acquiescence. Many hotels now make the traveling single woman feel less the lady of the night and more the woman executive. It is not with extra locks on the door that they are healing the problem. Rather, it is their attitude that has changed. The strange looks often encountered by the woman who checks in alone are fast disappearing— as it should.

However, these alterations in the attitudes of the business community are not the real problem. Instead, the honest woman will recognize that in the final analysis, these gestures are but necessary cosmetics to make life a little bit easier. And let's face it, they are good business practice. The larger questions rest in the hands of women, whose personal values, interpersonal relationships, and life-styles necessitate change and accommodation. There are practical and emotional factors to recognize. Each will be dealt with separately.

PRACTICAL PROBLEMS OF SUCCESS

If one day, upon arriving at your office, there are enough phone messages waiting for you to necessitate two hours of solitary conversation; if you're scheduled to attend a nephew's christening at the same time you're penciled in to make a speech to the Women's Marketing Executive Club in Duluth, Minnesota; should you feel a mild headache as a result of not being able to graciously say no to the sales manager of Ohio Plate, Inc., who insisted on just one more for the road before signing the contract; and if you have turned down the invitation to dinner (for the third time) and wonder if the story of having to visit a sick friend still holds up, then you are in the midst of the typical coping-with-success syndrome.

Privacy

One of the maxims of success is that everyone likes a winner. And everyone wants a piece of the winner. It is more than the insurance salesman or that man from the prestigious brokerage firm who will want your ear. These things are to be expected. Indeed, if you have made or intend to make your mark in the area of personal sales, you will readily sympathize with the needs of the salesperson to concentrate efforts on where the most likely action is. The most difficult problem to handle is the invasion of privacy by those seeking to benefit from the positive rub-off that friendship with a winner offers. The best way to cope with this is first to be aware that there are many whose motivations are less than sincere. The successful woman must guard against them. It's best to set up a specific time to see people and then to keep to the schedule. This method allows a structured atmosphere for the exposure of the successful woman to what may turn out to be new ideas. The virtues of limiting such intrusive periods will be self-evident. In general, it is best not to overschedule yourself. Anyone—even the ablest manager of time—can be done in by excesses of input. And the successful person will need, most of all, private moments in which to do nothing but think.

Marriage

Whether your view of contemporary marriage is a romantic one, a pragmatic one, or not yet fully defined, it is reasonable to assume that viewing this relationship from the practical point of view of the full-time, gainfully employed participants is a necessity. Two open-minded individuals serve as only the beginning of the answer to the problems posed by the working marriage. For example, one must be prepared to deal with the burdens that may come to the marriage as a result of disparity in income achievement and career achievement of the two partners. This is obviously a problem when the tradition of the male as breadwinner is challenged by the superior accomplishment of the female member. If women and men do not view themselves as being in competition in the earnings race, then the task of handling income differences will be made easier. What is important to remember is that each of the partners in the marriage is in some way (emotionally, sexually, supportively, financially, or intellectually) indispensable to the other partner. If one understands that money cannot buy what is commonly referred to as happiness, then the matter of career achievement will not be a problem.

THANK GOD IT'S FRIDAY.   She lives in Washington, D.C., and he's a New York resident. Every other Friday one or the other of them boards a plane and begins a journey to two and one-half days of marital bliss. Each summer they manage to take their vacations together, and for that purpose their six-figure income has provided a shared country hideaway at the seashore. What keeps these modern explorers of a new kind of marriage together? Well, for one thing, the convenience of jet aircraft travel helps. The other factors are far more subjective but no less important. They have made the decision to postpone having children for the time being. So it is an easy task to close up their respective apartments and simply be on the road. Friends play a part also. Our contemporary marriage partners have established a network of relationships that sustain them as individuals when they are apart and support them as a couple when they are together. And the future sustains them also. Each of the partners in this very unusual marriage is aware that nothing is forever, and that one day their plan to be together always will mature into a reality. One of the two of them will have managed that job transfer or job switch to a company located in the same city as the partner, or perhaps one will decide that it is his or her role to end the accumulation of income and seek a job whose geographic demands place no strains on the marriage. It is not always pleasant to live so far from the one you love; however, it is manageable. One must be strong, though, to accomplish such an undertaking. It is not for everyone. In my case, we are both based in New York, but there are weeks during which it may well be an East Coast-West Coast situation. Between us both traveling, working late, and having dinner appointments, there are many weeks where one of us stumbles in the door, exhausted, at bedtime and barely has more than ten minutes' conversation for the day.

Dealing with Tall, Dark, and Deadly

I have no desire, nor do I feel unusually competent, to offer advice on the matter of handling the sexual pressures that all of us have, at one time or another, found to be an inevitable part of the job. The subject is only included in this chapter because it is the experience of many that it is an area in which one may well be called upon to develop certain coping armaments. Notwithstanding the avowed management policies which implicitly forbid, and even threaten with discipline, those who would by means of blackmail imply that sexual favors proffered will lead to promotion and other rewards, it is the practical experience of many women that such policies serve better to protect the corporation and its reputation than they do to protect its women employees. The only way to cope with such pressure is directly. If an uncalled-for pressure is felt, then it is best to confront the antagonist and clear the air. It is suggested that one's position vis à vis the extramarital affair be clearly spelled out. If this does not do the job, then better to find out now. It's time to seek other employment.

Two-Martini Lunches

The entire area of alcohol as it affects the successful woman is, of course, a very personal one. I choose to let the statistics speak for themselves. Fully 10 percent of the American adult population has trouble handling alcohol. The successful woman will find herself much in demand, and the crossover between business and social occasions is a constant factor in the American business scene. At the top of the heap, the successful woman will be feted, courted, sought out, and generally exposed to the splendors and the excesses of the good life. American businesses acknowledge that $10 billion annually is the cost to industry of the alcohol-dependent executive. Major corporations attempt to control such problems by frowning upon those who drink to excess, providing psychiatric counsel and other such rehabilitative techniques. Dealing with the two-martini lunch is no less a problem for the successful woman than it is for the successful man. Personally, I'm grateful to the popularity of bottled water. I can now order a nonalcoholic drink without the client or waiter frowning.

EMOTIONAL FACTORS AND SUCCESS

Perhaps more complex than these practical problems just covered is the entire area of emotional problems which will be new territory for the woman who has made it. Success does have its price tag. The problems associated with it may seem, at worst, irritants with no deeper impact. Dealing with a series of subtle changes in one's life-style can have a cumulative negative effect. And this is the area that should be understood so one can guard against it.

Denying the Past

The euphoria that often accompanies success in the business world brings with it the quick rush that is the winner's experience. The adrenaline pumps harder as the business press encircles the winner, eager for the story. Often it's a rags-to-riches story, completely unprecedented and completely unplanned. Even for the successful woman whose dreams come true as a result of unusual competence and original skills, the element of luck will more than likely have entered into the process of winning. Sometimes, though—and seemingly all too often—the shred of modesty that distinguishes the truly sage executive from the stereotypical, flip, even brash one has somewhere been lost in the difficult battle to the top of the heap. Cosmetic gestures can transform the woman executive into a model of fashion excellence. Communications training can eliminate telltale speech habits which she may see as not being worthy of her new station in life. Indeed, an entire series of image-transformation activities can be undertaken, all of which will bring our successful woman more in line with the image of success that the media dictates is "in." These activities are all well and good, at worst harmless, with one possible and very important exception. For that woman who has made it and has chosen to forget her roots, the image transformation can be an unsettling and dangerous experience. Psychologists tell us that basic personality changes are not within the desirable province of their fine art. There are too few genuine psychic roots that keep our feet on the ground as it is. The woman who seeks to hide her origins, alter her thinking to conform to that picture of success she thinks she must live up to, is in grave danger of losing altogether those very same personality traits that no doubt were instrumental in bringing her to a position of business preeminence.

The bonding mechanism that operates to cement relationships between friends and friendships of long standing is probably the best guard against this erosion of the old perspective to the circumstances that will surround success. A history of shared experiences during one's formative years has the effect of bringing things back to basics. Pretense and affectation are not allowed within the definition of most true friendships. The relationship of the successful businesswoman with those who "knew her when" allows the executive to let down her defenses and find, once again, the person she really is.

On Top and Alone

For many good reasons, and some not so good, the successful executive too often finds that standing astride the limited territory found at the top of the business pyramid has the effect of cutting the executive off from those who had made the arduous journey with her. This process has two damaging effects. The loneliness that all too often accompanies the success-oriented executive has a debilitating emotional effect. She can feel isolated, unwanted, underutilized. The cost in human terms is catastrophic. Few people are strong enough to be entirely self-sufficient. All need a structure for life, some means for feedback and interrelationships so that one is able to see where one fits into the greater scheme of things. The structure is defined by those institutions in which we place our emotional investment: family, business organization, friends, schools, government, church, and the like. The executive who comes through the combat of corporate interplay, who has successfully bested her peers, will find the need to carry with her some intimates who can share her newfound laurels.

Isolation has a secondary effect which is also negative. The successful executive can all too easily begin to place credence in the validity of her own press notices. So doing, she begins to live up to the image that others have no doubt chosen for her. In the process, she begins to lose touch with the practical circumstances of the business world whose previous appreciation has in many cases been responsible, or at least contributed to her success. Key customer contacts are avoided. The isolation-prone executive tends to rely more on written information than the verbal back-and-forth touch of face-to-face conversations with real people in real situations.

The description of the set of offices that are the special territory of the woman at the top as the executive suite is not one that has been come to capriciously. A suite is defined as being of "related things." Contemporary business leaders are finding daily that the limitations they erroneously feel are placed on their personnel contacts down the line are self-defeating. Today's leader sees herself in a different light. She must be ahead of her followers, in touch with her followers, dependent on her followers, appreciative of her followers, protective of her followers, and inspired by her followers. There is no room for one-dimensional rarefied thinking.

Children

The responsibilities of family tug at the heartstrings of the successful woman. Excepting those women for whom motherhood holds no fascination, the management of children in a career-oriented family structure is the most difficult task the successful woman will have to cope with. Absence for long periods of time, the need to surrogate much of the time needed for the child's development to someone else, and the management of those guilt feelings that are often a part of the successful mother's overly divided life, all play a part. There are no hard and firm rules available for the management of this problem. One would hope to be able to do more than just cope with motherhood. It is too early in the development of the woman in the business cycle to actually know what effect the denial of motherhood, or its surrogation, will have. It is a difficult problem area which, at best, we can experiment with.

Financial Counsel

The successful woman will one day take inventory of her accomplishments and note to her surprise that the list of assets she has accumulated will be considerable. If finance is not her own specialized area of interest, the retention of financial counsel is indicated. Going beyond the obvious need to have tax assistance, it is the management of the entire scope of the successful woman's financial affairs that can be affected. Long-range financial planning seeks as its goal the management of money and other assets for growth. Proper investment counsel is available to the woman executive as part of the services of most major banks. Their current and most sensible approach is the so-called total package money management school. Banks handle tax matters, insurance, investment, mortgage money, loans, and a variety of credit arrangements. They also advise on securities portfolios, pension and welfare situations, tax shelters, gifts to children, and many other matters. The independent financial counselor has also come into the picture in recent years. Such persons usually work closely with banks to arrange lines of credit and, in general, carry out many of these same functions. With the time demands on the successful executive being as stringent as they are likely to be, the retention of outside financial counsel is a vitally important matter.

Legal Counsel

In a land of laws, it may sometimes seem that the law operates not to protect the innocent but to confuse him or her. Be that as it may, the intricacies of the law as it affects the estate, assets, tax base, marriage, responsibilities of business ownership, and a thousand and one other facets of business life are not always best left to the judgment of the successful and busy executive. The success-oriented woman will do well to retain good legal counsel. The choice often depends on the specific areas of specialty required by the executive. Notwithstanding the conservative tilt of the American electorate, the day of less rather than more government involvement in both business and personal affairs does not loom just over the horizon. Women, their rights, equities, and privileges are well serviced by wise and commited counsel.

Family Counsel

The successful executive has probably already noted that the art of coping involves keeping on even terms with something. In this case, one hopes to keep on even terms with success. Implicit in such a definition is the understanding that it is an ongoing and difficult task. One is happy to be able to stay even, no less to get ahead of success. The task is doubly difficult for women, for all the previously noted reasons. There is little in the way of a framework against which to lean for guidance. The entire area of success, and women who are successful, is for the most part uncharted. There is but a small body of experience. However, there is a considerable ally available to women and those who share their new-found success in the form of the professional counselor, whether clergyman, therapist, human relations expert, close friend, or relative. That person who can act as a confidential sounding board for the successful woman can be a powerful asset.

SURE SIGNS THAT YOU'VE MADE IT

As you have probably already discovered, there are certain prerogatives that go with success. In addition to all those things which the successful woman will have to cope with, there is indeed a good deal to be enjoyed.

Feeling that perhaps the more positive side of success should have an airing, I have compiled a list of sure signs of success. One is advised to take somewhat irreverent guidelines in the lighthearted manner in which they are intended. A short coffee break is in order.

1. At a luncheon to which you were invited, if you pick up the check because you feel you're better able to afford it than your host, then you have arrived.

2. If you find yourself saying, "My first available free day is August 26," and the first of July hasn't yet arrived, then you've arrived.

3. If you feel they shot your "bad side" in that trade-journal profile on your climb to success—well, you've made it.

4. If you dash down handwritten notes on memo stationary marked "From the Desk of," then you've arrived.

5. If you choose the hundred-thousand-mile lounge of the airport and hang an elegant, if casual, airplane identification sticker on your over-night luggage, then you've arrived.

6. If you bring your grocer, dry cleaner, hairdresser, and travel bills to the office and have portions of them written off against your expense account, then you've arrived.

7. If your opinions about the economy, international affairs, the price of gold and the inflation/unemployment trade-off are frequently solicited, then you've arrived.

8. If fruit and flowers sit at the dressing table of your hotel room, then you've arrived.

9. If your mother calls to say she will agree to take the children for the entire Labor Day weekend so that you and your husband can have some time to reacquaint yourselves with one another, then you know you've arrived.

10. If you are asked to deliver a speech to a group of colleagues on the subject of Coping with Success, then you know you've arrived.

Success is, to a certain degree, a self-fulfilling process. Given the competitive nature of the society in which we live, attitudes and commitment must be harnessed and channeled in a disciplined manner. It is, of course, a question of individual choice. Some will prefer to risk the climb. Others—and there are many—will avoid it. Obviously, it is all a relative matter. Being aware of the nature of the arena into which the success-oriented woman will, of necessity, have to enter is a rational approach to making that difficult decision that will lead women inextricably through a labyrinth of challenging, difficult, and oftentimes rewarding experiences.

Postscript

Marketing is by no means the only answer. The professions, the arts, government, the political arena, indeed all arenas, should beckon to today's woman. We, all of us, have a unique opportunity. The experience of the women's movement, more than anything else, should be proof enough for the woman who seeks to chart new waters. Ten years ago, one hesitated. The conditioning of society has made most women doubt the soundness of their own ideas, the merits of their own credibility. Today, these psychic barriers have been lifted. Now a more difficult arena is entered. Women must be able to perform now that freedom is here. There is no room for a woman in business who would hide behind her own skirts. The establishment, fighting to the last, has been forced to give us our opportunity. We must be prepared—in most cases, better prepared than our male peers. The American economy, the conditions of the world, will certainly benefit from such growth.

Index

Professional associations, 151–52
Professional Ethics, 65
Professional service organizations, and
  marketing, 64–73
  concepts of, 68
  consultants and, 64, 66–73
    benefits of, 69–70
    case history of, 68–71
    retention of, 71–72
  contracts, 73
  fee structuring, 72
  overhead, 72
Profits, and sales efforts, 42
Psychiatrists, business, 134
Public relations, 9–10, 58, 61, 62
Publishing, in marketing, 153–54
  trade publications, 153–54

Quotas, for sales, 38–39

Retailing business, 12
Revlon, Inc., case history of, 46–48
Risk-taking, 83–84, 175

Sales Executive Club, 152
Sales & Marketing Management, 153
Sales, new product, 23
Salespeople, 35–36
  evaluation of, 39
  and sales organizations, 40–42
  See also Selling, personal
Sales promotion, 9, 26–34, 58, 62, 107–9, 122
  as entry-level field, 107–9
  incentives for, 32–33
  planning programs, 33–34
  strategy for, 120
  techniques of, 27–34
    advertising specialties, 29
    audiovisual presentations, 31
    business meetings, 32
    direct mail, 30
    point of purchase displays, 31–32
    premiums, 27–28
    printing production, 31
    promotion/space advertising, 31
    sweepstakes, 29–30
    trade shows/exhibits, 30
  See also Marketing, case histories
Savin Business Machines, case history of, 53–54
Self-image, 82, 85–86
Selling, personal, 35–44, 103–7
  as entry-level field, 103–7
  evaluation, 39–40
  feedback, 38
  five steps of, 37
  future of, 43–44
  incentive system, 39
  and profits, 42–43
  quotas, 38–39
  selling structures, 40–42
Selling structures, 40–42
Service businesses, 13

Socializing, peer/colleague, 152–53
Society of Security Analysts, The, 152
Sperry Rand Corporations, 102
Standard Industry Classification Code (SIC), 51
Stereotypical images, 83, 87–88
Strategy for Success, A, 163–64
Success:
  checklist for, 167–68
  coping with, 163–64, 197–206
  emotional factors, 202–5
  fear of, 79–80
  predicting, 87–95
    drives, 90–95
    personality assessment, 87–90
  problems of, 199–202
    business lunches, 201–202
    marriage, 200–201
    privacy, 199–200
    sexual pressures, 201
  signs of, 205–6
Survival techniques, 139–49
  corporate etiquette, 147–49
  criticism, 142
  during a meeting, examples, 140–43
  strategic exiting, 143
Sutton, Willie, 198
Sweepstakes, as a sales promotion tool, 29–30

Tangibility, as a market value, 67
Testing, product or service, 6–7, 15, 21, 23
  concept test, 21
Trade publications, 153–54
Trade shows, 30

Vlasic Foods, case history, 498–49
Volunteer organizations, 61

Wall Street Journal, The, 161
Weight Watchers, 33
*Who Gets Ahead? The Determinants of Economic
  Success*, 167
Wilson, Charles, 173
Wittench, Warren J., 67
Women:
  as business owners, 173–85
  career advancement in marketing, 150–59
  executive status, 160–69
  in industry, 15
  influence of, 4
  interviews, 157–59
  juggling career, marriage, family, 186–96
  marketing as career for, 12–15, 77–84, 85–98,
    99–109
  networking, 157
  in nonprofit marketing, 63
  in personal sales, 35–44
  self-image, 82
  survival techniques for, 139–49
  success, coping with, 163–64, 197–206
  See also Business ownership; Families,
    two-career; Marketing, career strategy
Workaholic, 91

Xerox corporation, 53–54